O, SAY CAN U C?

A Hidden Letter Alphabet Book — Written & Illustrated by Bradd Parton

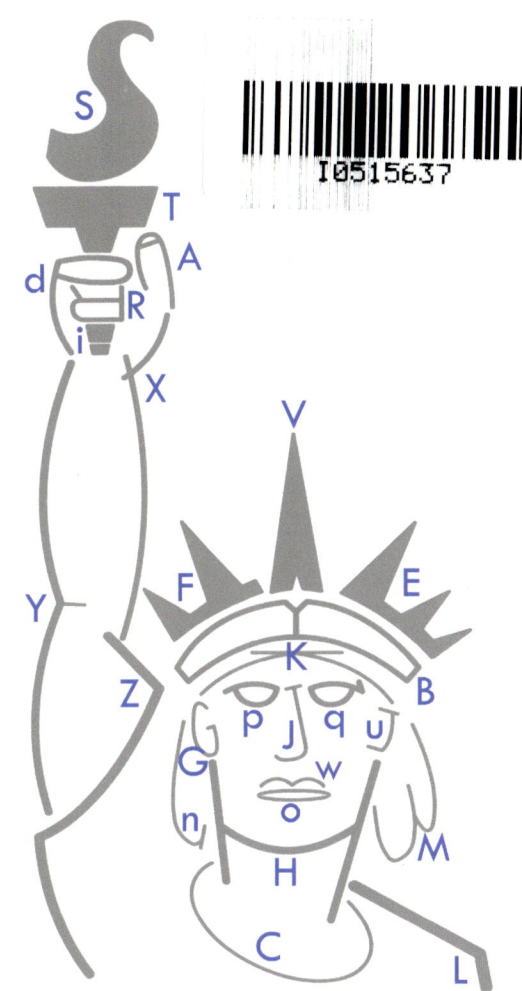

ABOUT THE ART

All illustrations in this book were drawn with the Alpha-Sketch technique. The author created this style where every line is a letter of the alphabet, and each letter is used once in the drawing. There are no omissions, repetitions, or extra lines.

Each illustration is decoded in the back of the book just like the Statue of Liberty to the right.

Have fun finding the letters!

No portion of this book may be used or reproduced in any manner whatsoever without the written permission of the author. The scanning, uploading, and distribution of this book via the Internet or any other means without the permission of the author is illegal and punishable by law. The prose, Alpha-Sketch technique, and the drawings herein including all related elements are trademarked and copyrighted by Bradd Parton. All rights reserved. O, SAY CAN U C? is copyright 2017. The illustrations in this book were created digitally.

website: www.braddparton.com
instagram: /alpha.sketch
shop: www.alpha-sketch.com
twitter: @bradd
e-mail: braddparton@gmail.com
facebook: /alphasketch

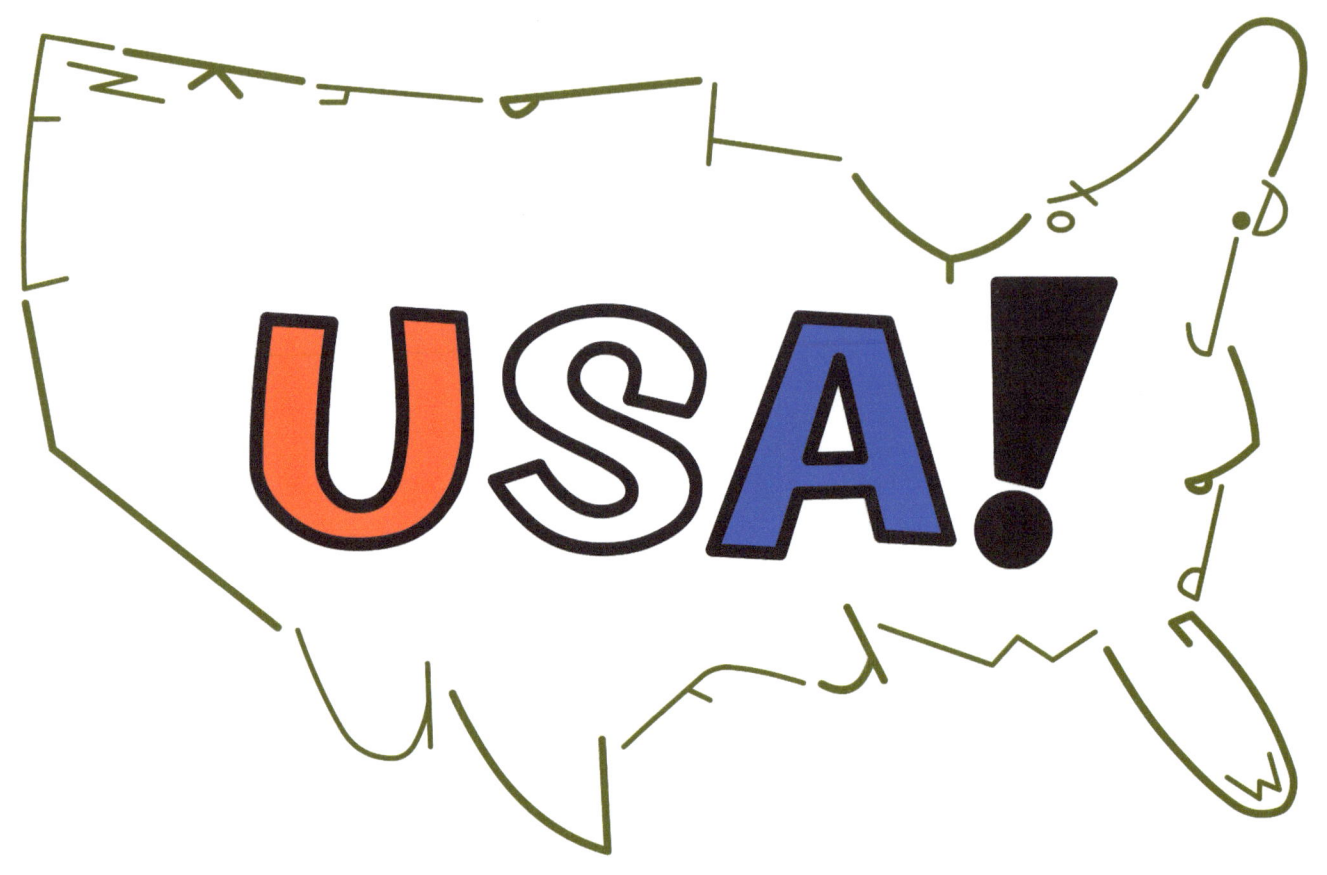

A is for America.
Our country has 50 states.
Listen and I'll share with you
Some great things, people, & dates.

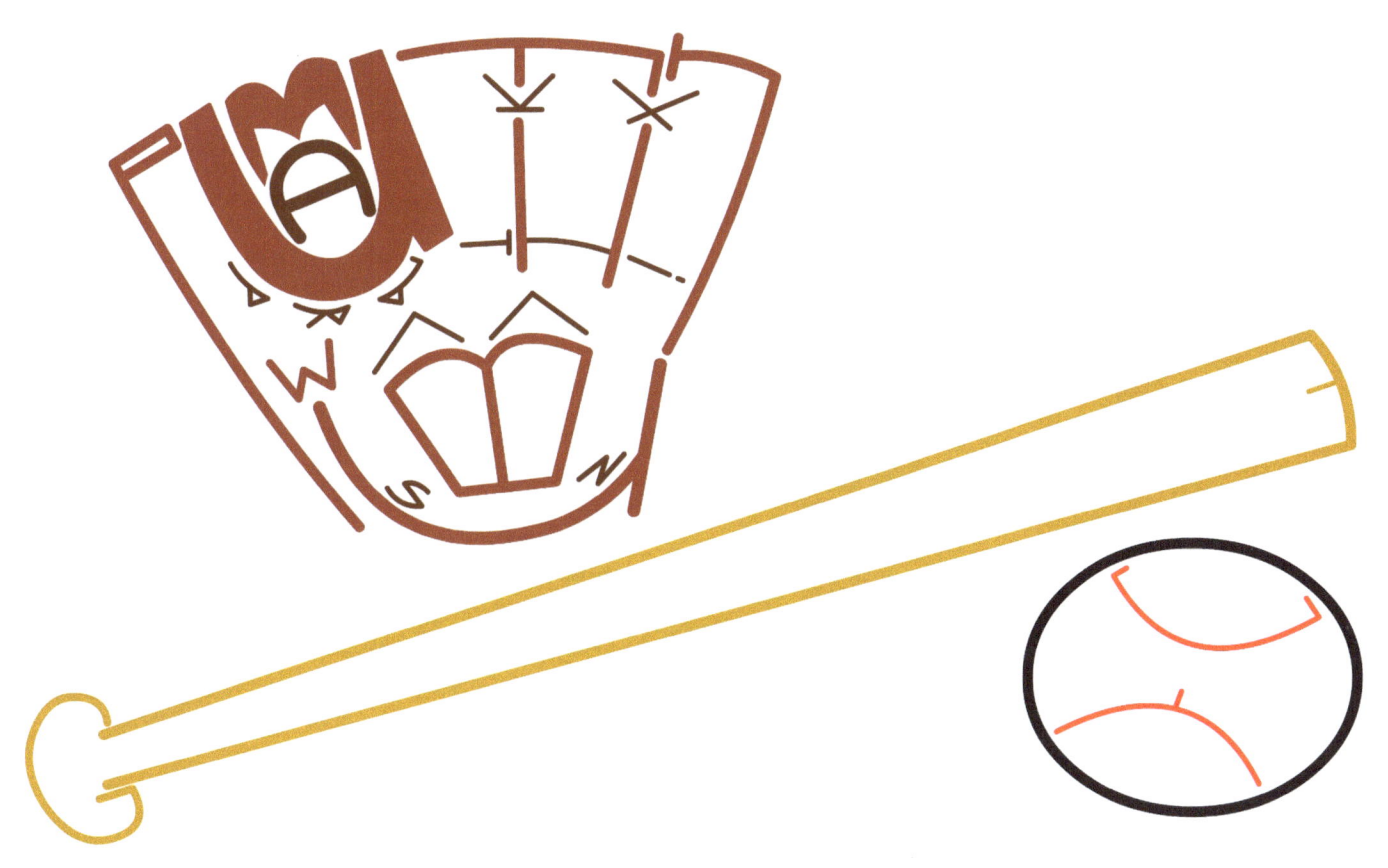

B is for baseball,
A truly American sport.
Hit the ball and run for first,
If you're the athletic sort.

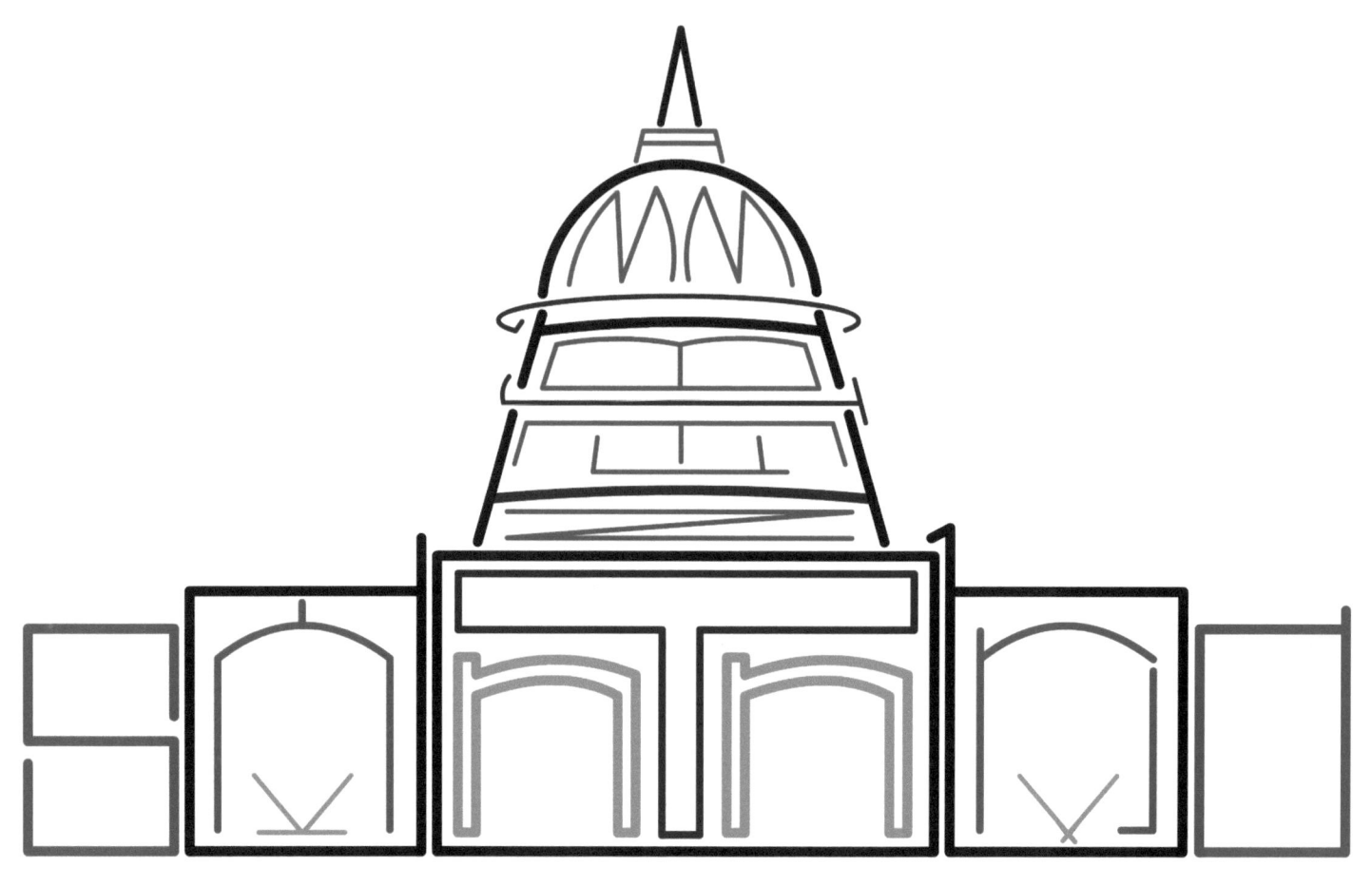

C is for the Capitol,
Built in 1793.
All of Congress works there
In Washington, D.C.

D is for the Declaration,
Where we claimed our independence.
It's similar to the Constitution,
But without all the Amendments.

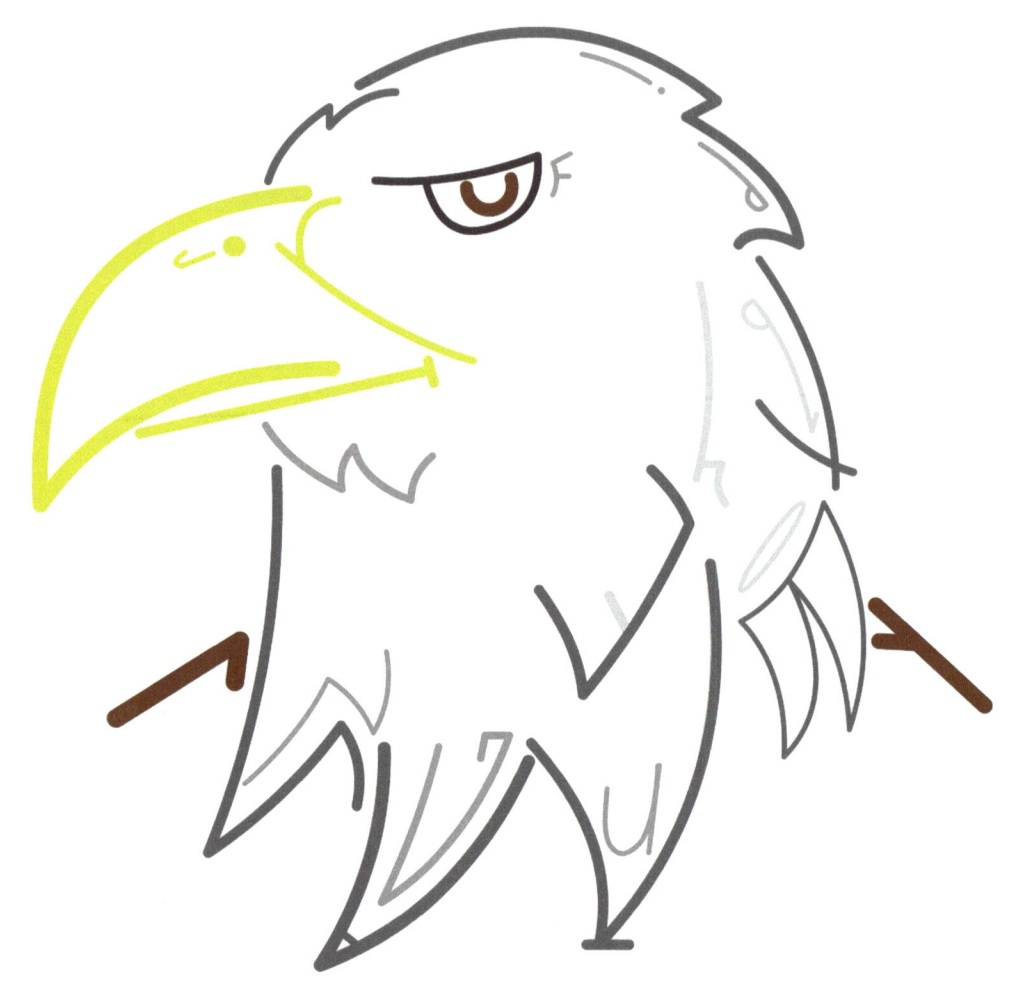

E is for the Eagle,
A symbol of the U.S.A.
Full of grace and dignity,
Flying strong, come what may.

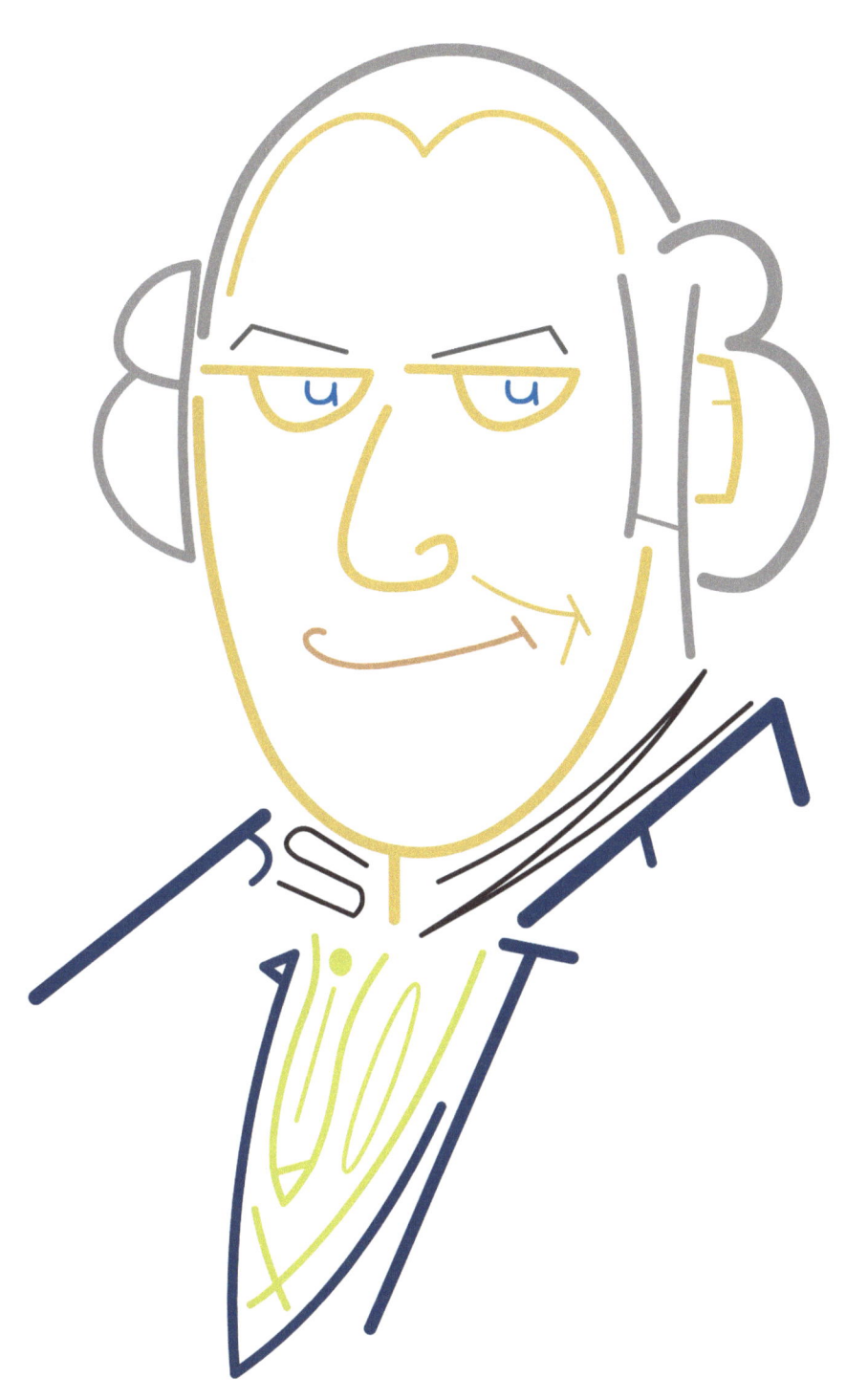

F is for our Founding Fathers,

Brave men who built this land.

Washington, Franklin, Hamilton, Adams,

And more all lent a hand.

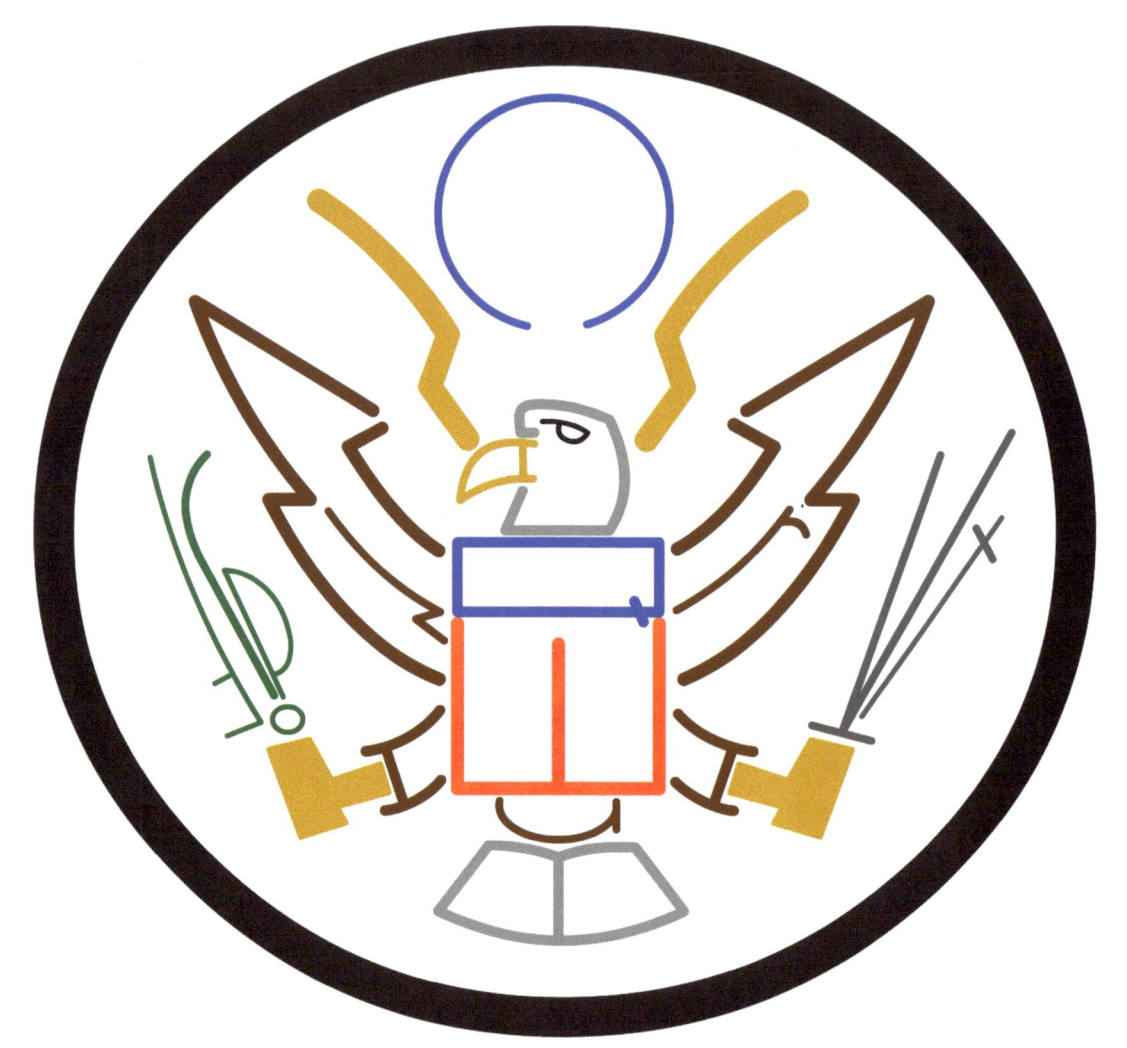

G is for the Great Seal,
Our national coat of arms or crest.
Lots of countries have one,
But I like ours the best.

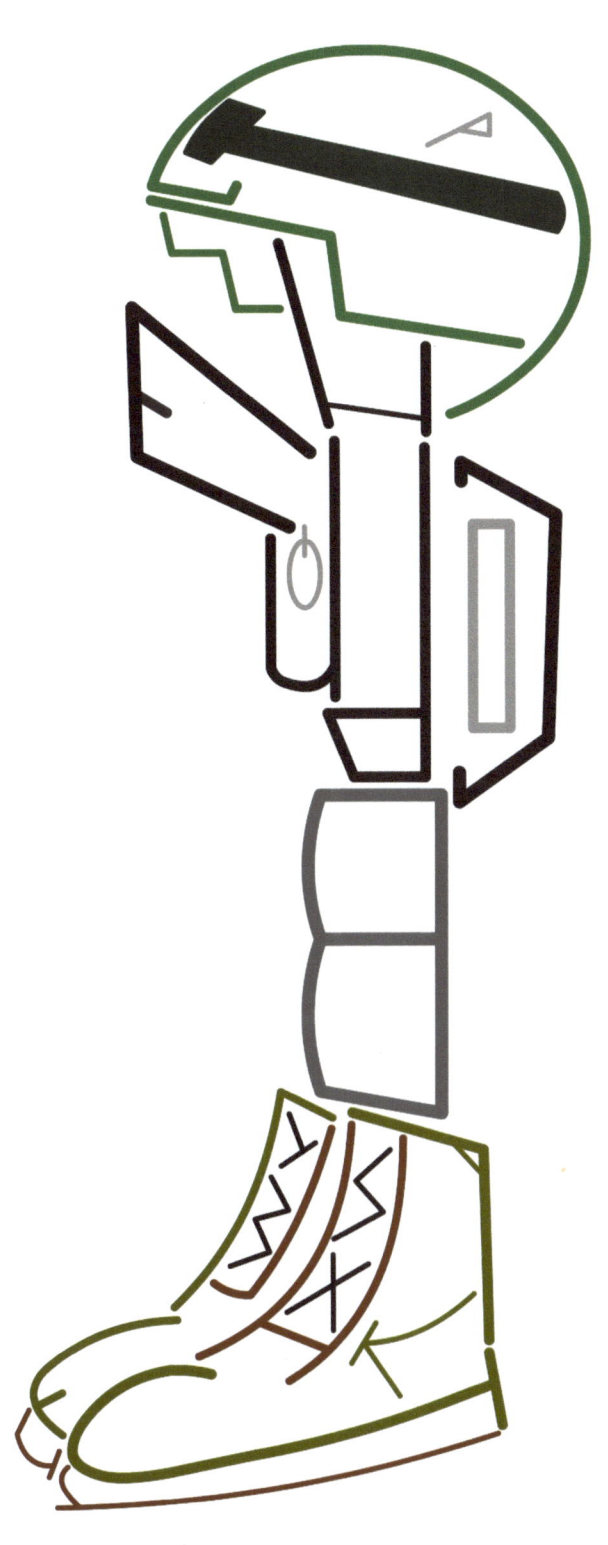

H is for "Home of the Brave."

Remember those who went to war.

Never forget those men and women

And what they were fighting for.

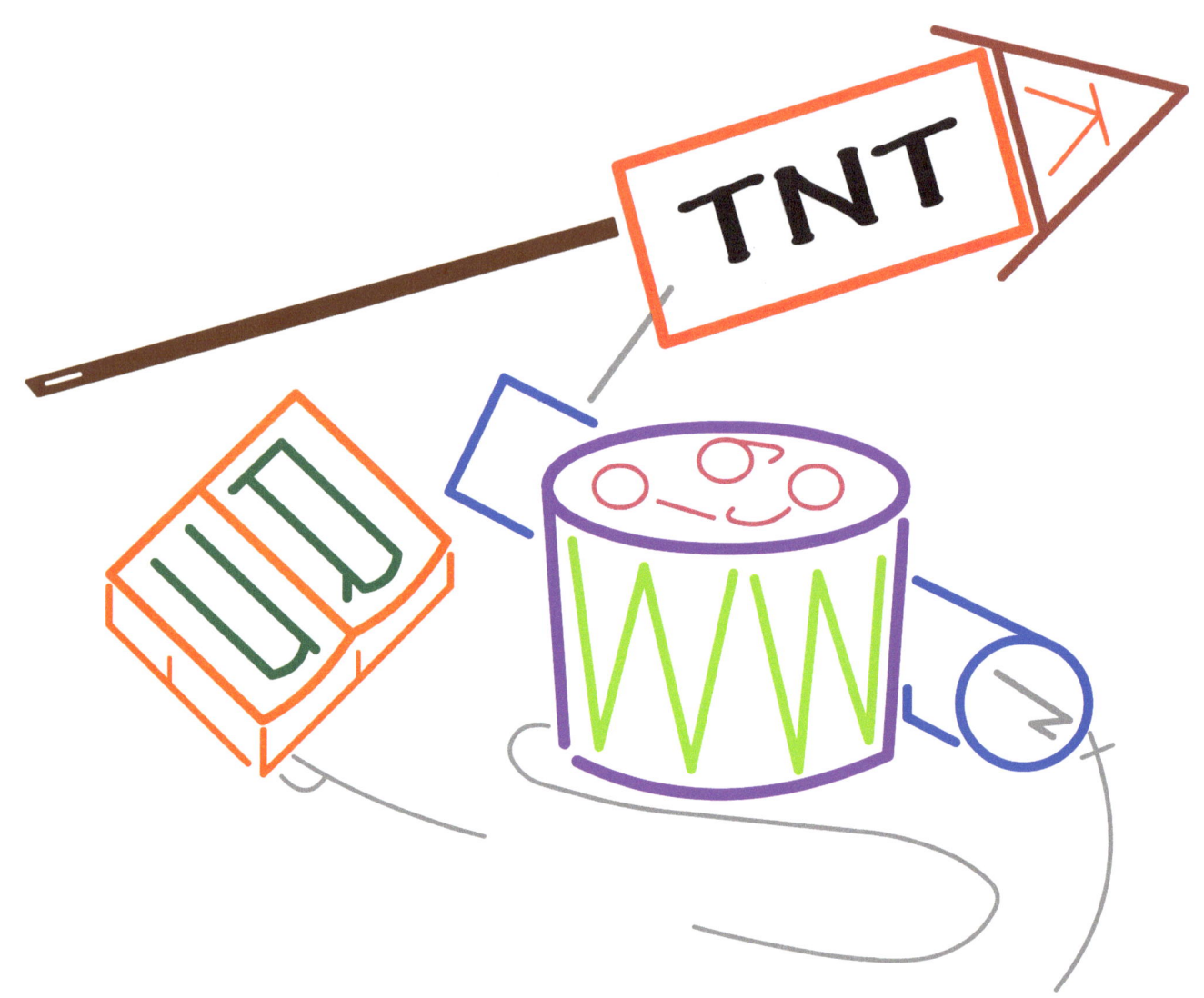

I is for Independence Day,
Celebrated on the 4th of July.
We're reminded of our history
As fireworks light up the sky.

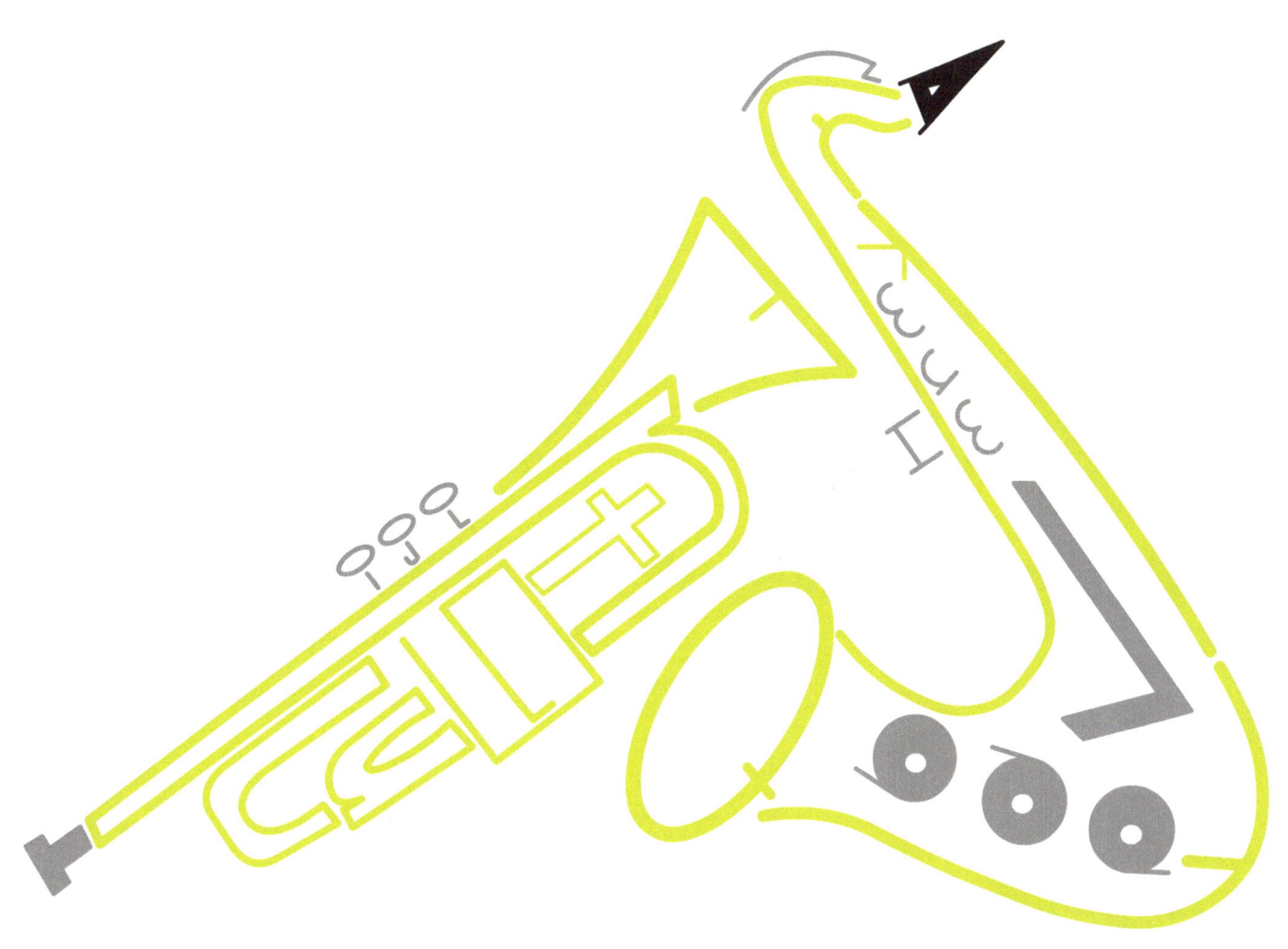

J is for Jazz,
An American musical style.
Whether swing, bop, or fusion,
This music makes me smile.

K is for Martin Luther King, Junior.

When it came to equality, he led the fight.

We've come a long way since King,

But we're still working to get it right.

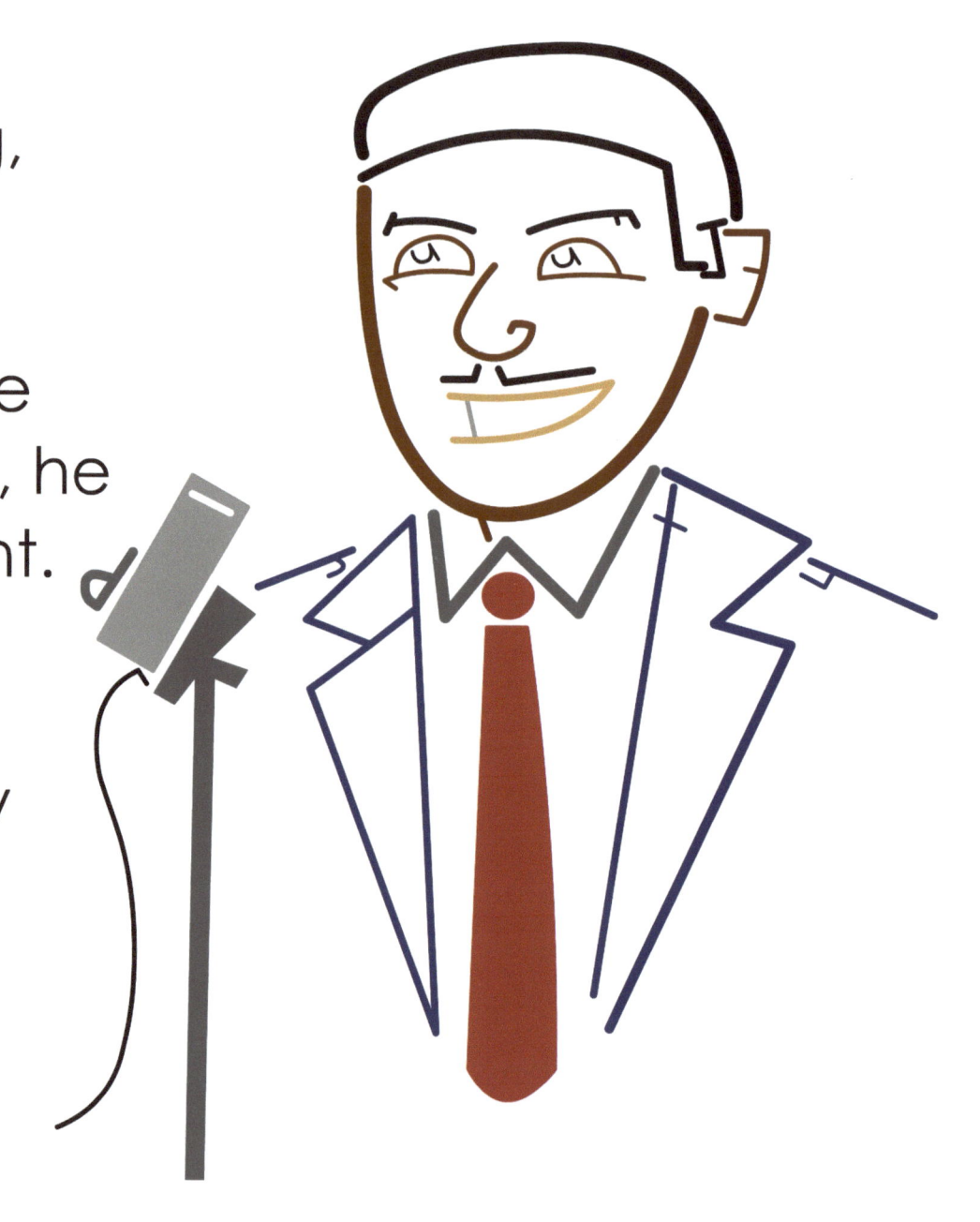

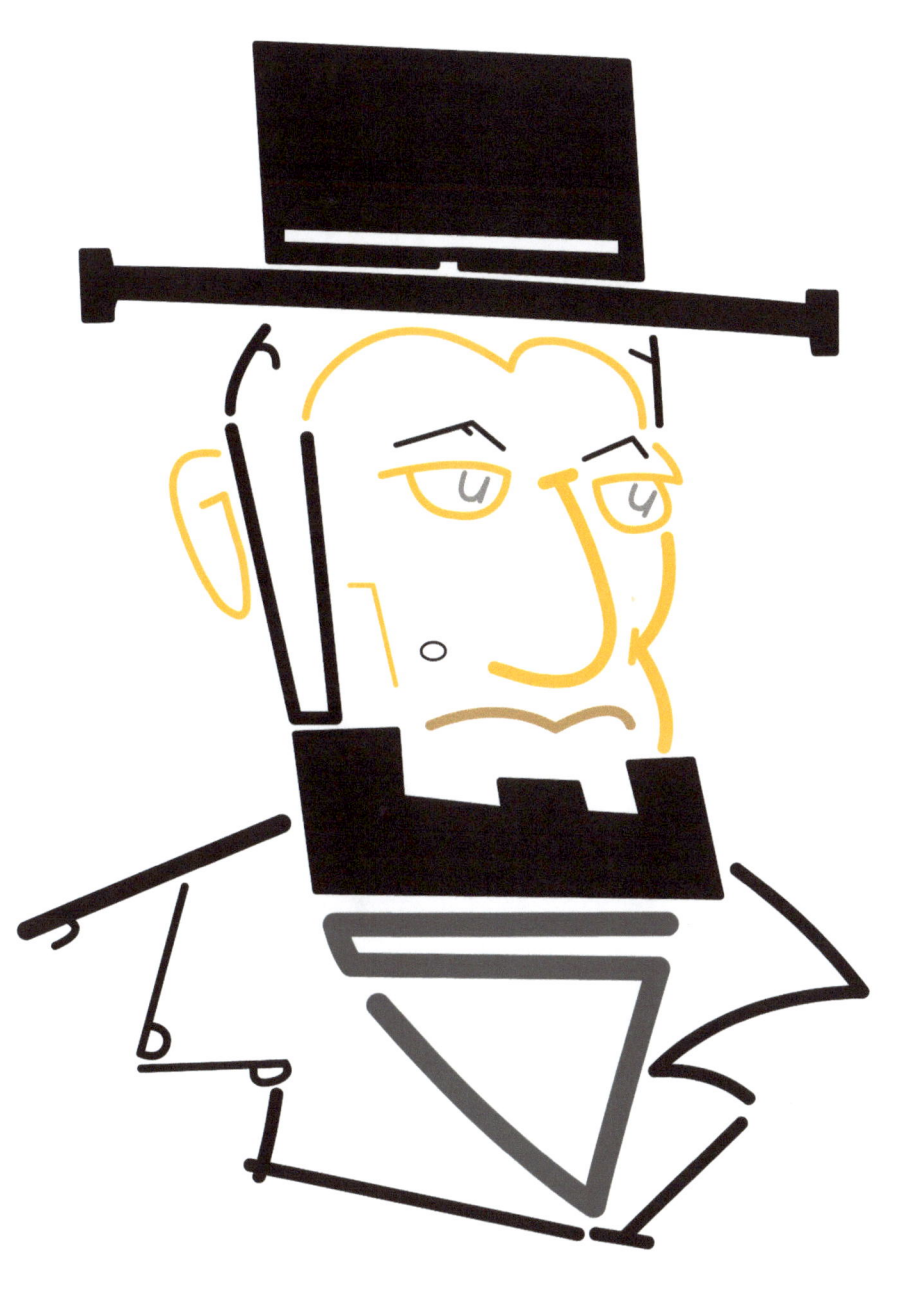

L is for Abraham Lincoln,

Our sixteenth President.

You'll find him on the penny,

A coin that's worth one cent.

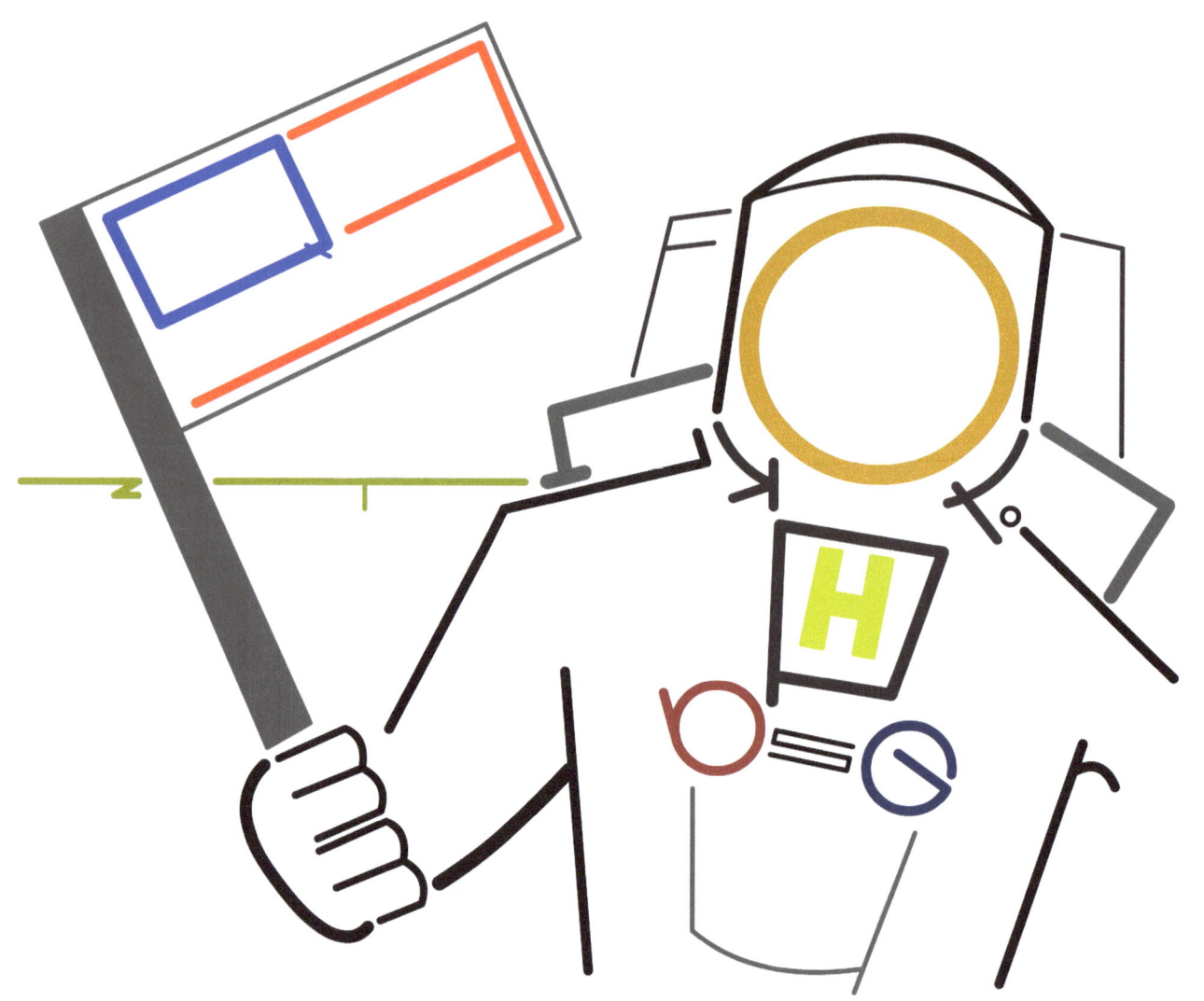

M is for the Moon Landing.
Apollo 11 touched down in '69.
Neil Armstrong's small step
Was a giant leap for mankind.

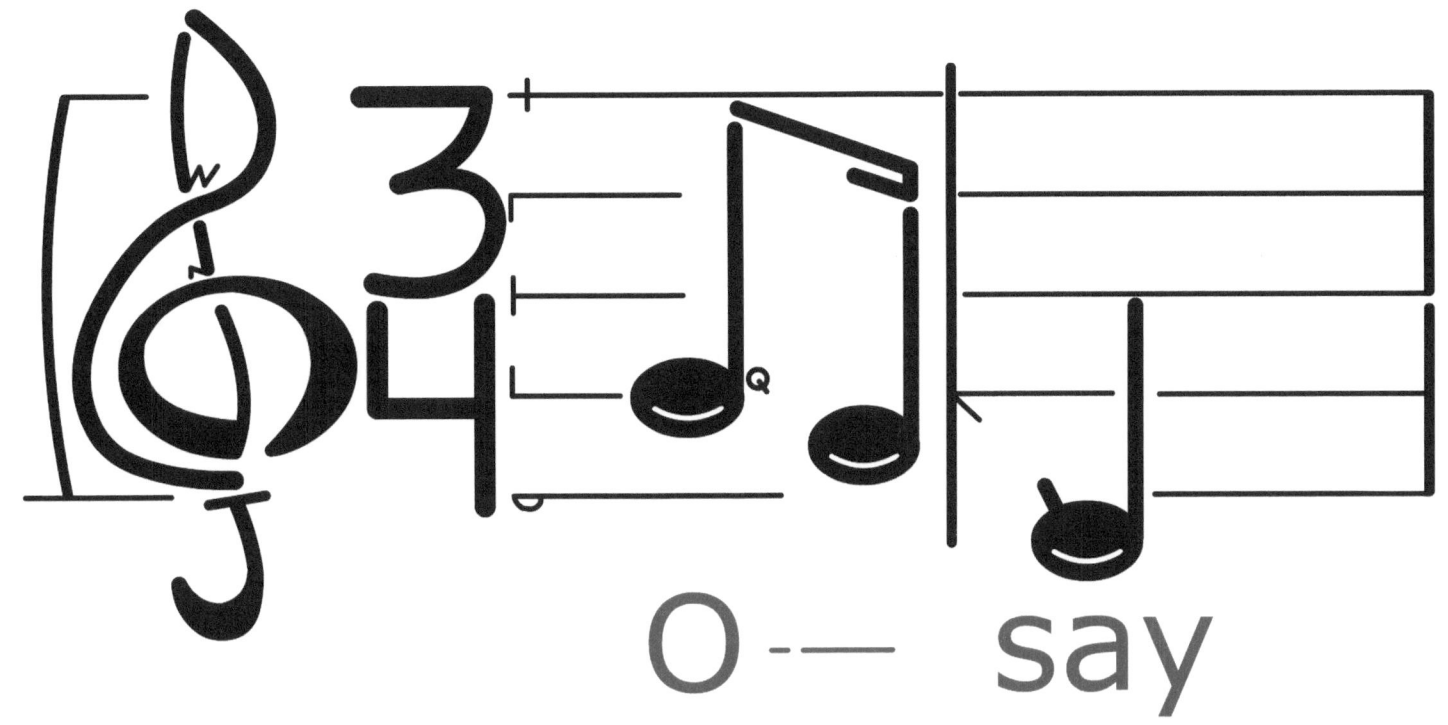

N is for the National Anthem
Written by Francis Scott Key.
It's called "The Star-Spangled Banner"
And starts with "O, Say Can You See?"

O is for
 Old Glory

With its
 stripes and
 fifty stars.

Every
 country
 has a flag,

And the red,
 white, and
 blue is ours.

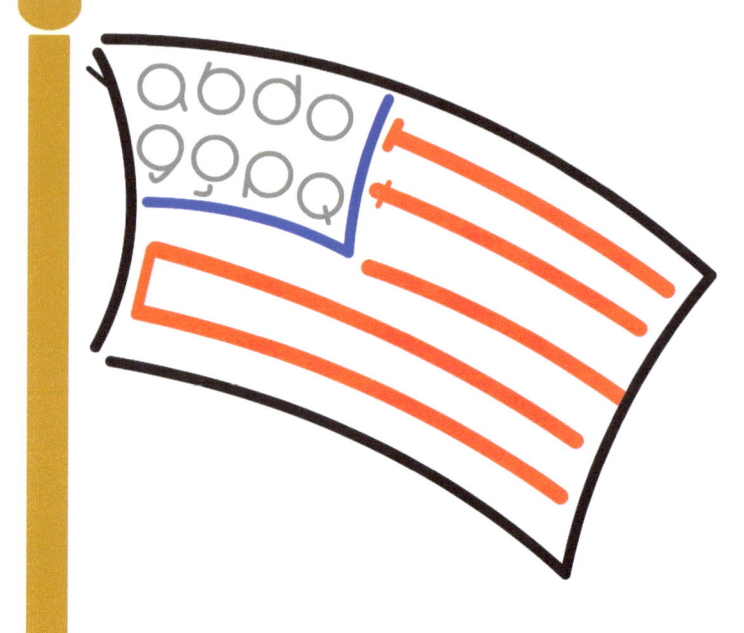

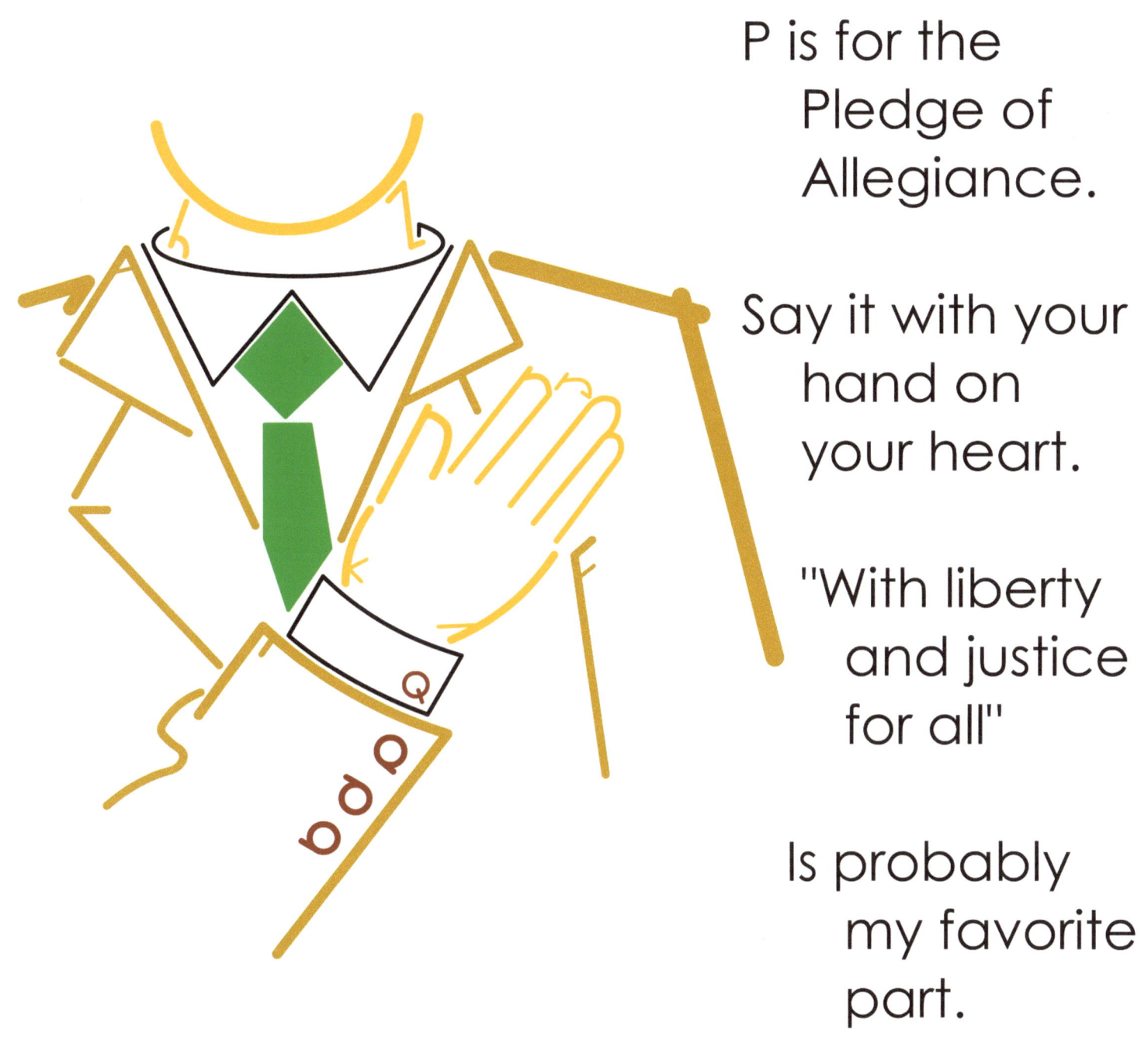

P is for the Pledge of Allegiance.

Say it with your hand on your heart.

"With liberty and justice for all"

Is probably my favorite part.

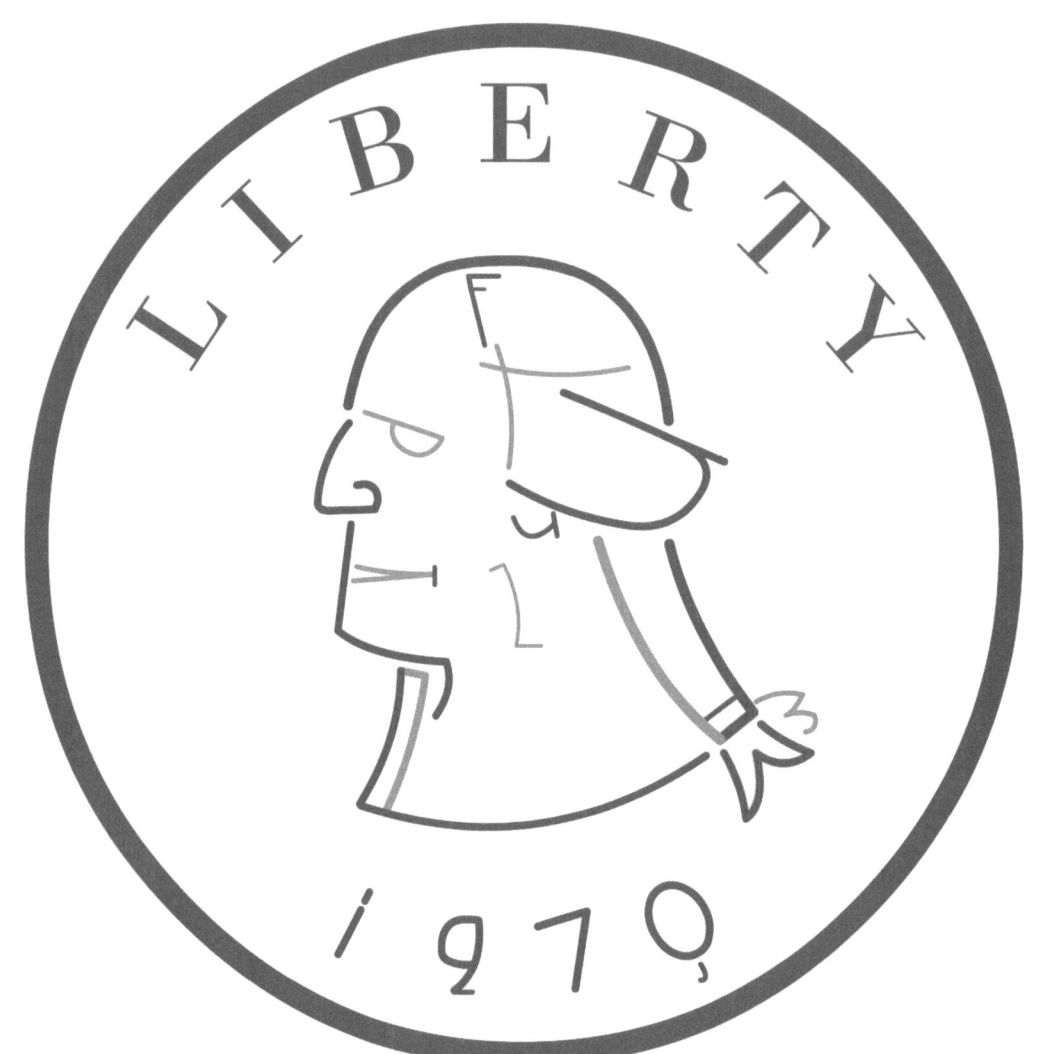

Q is for the Quarter,
And though I'm not a scholar,
Put four of them together
And then you'll have a dollar.

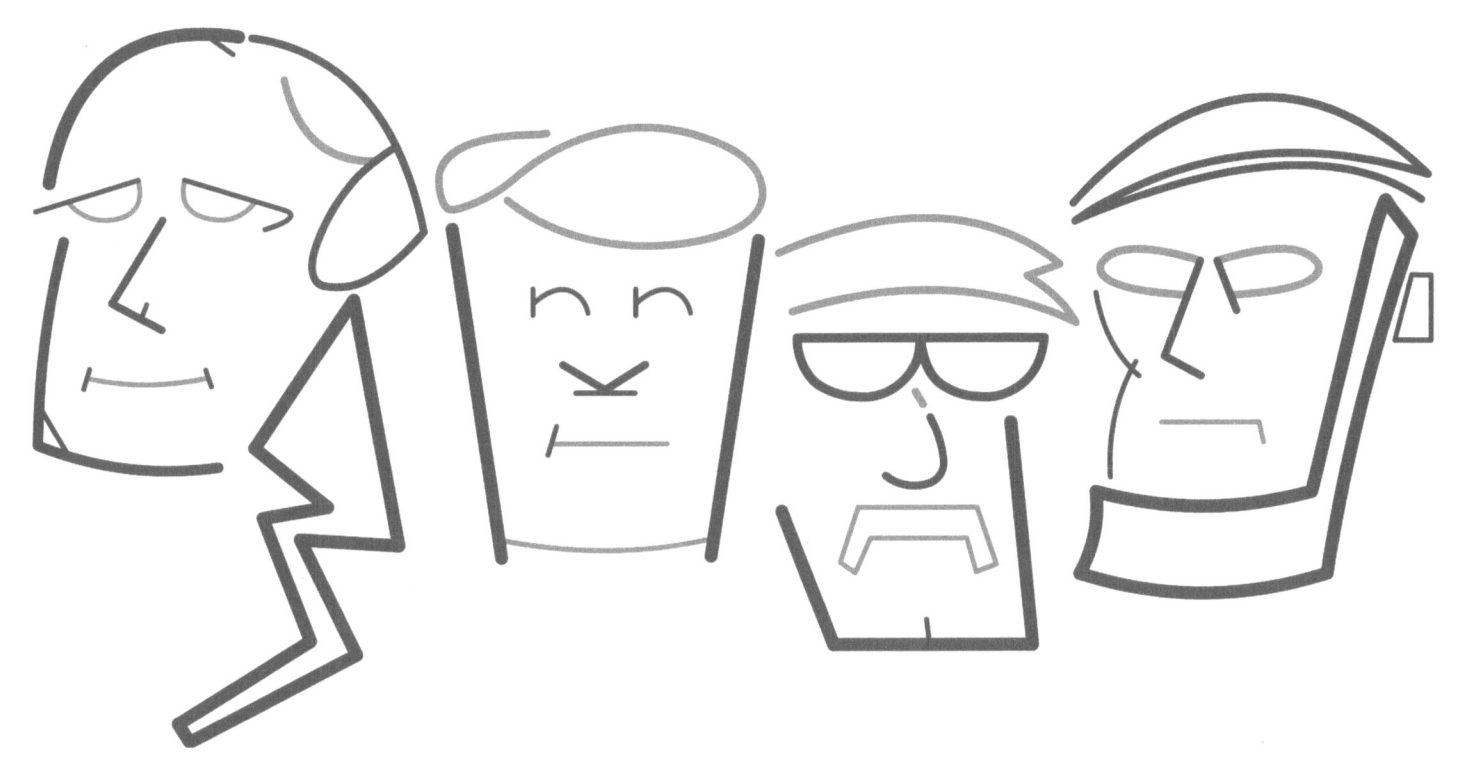

R is for Rushmore.
There's nothing like it on the planet.
Washington, Jefferson, Roosevelt & Lincoln
All carved in the mountain's granite.

S is for
   the Statue
   of Liberty.

She stands
   in New
   York City.

Thousands of
   immigrants
   agree

No other
   lady is
   as pretty.

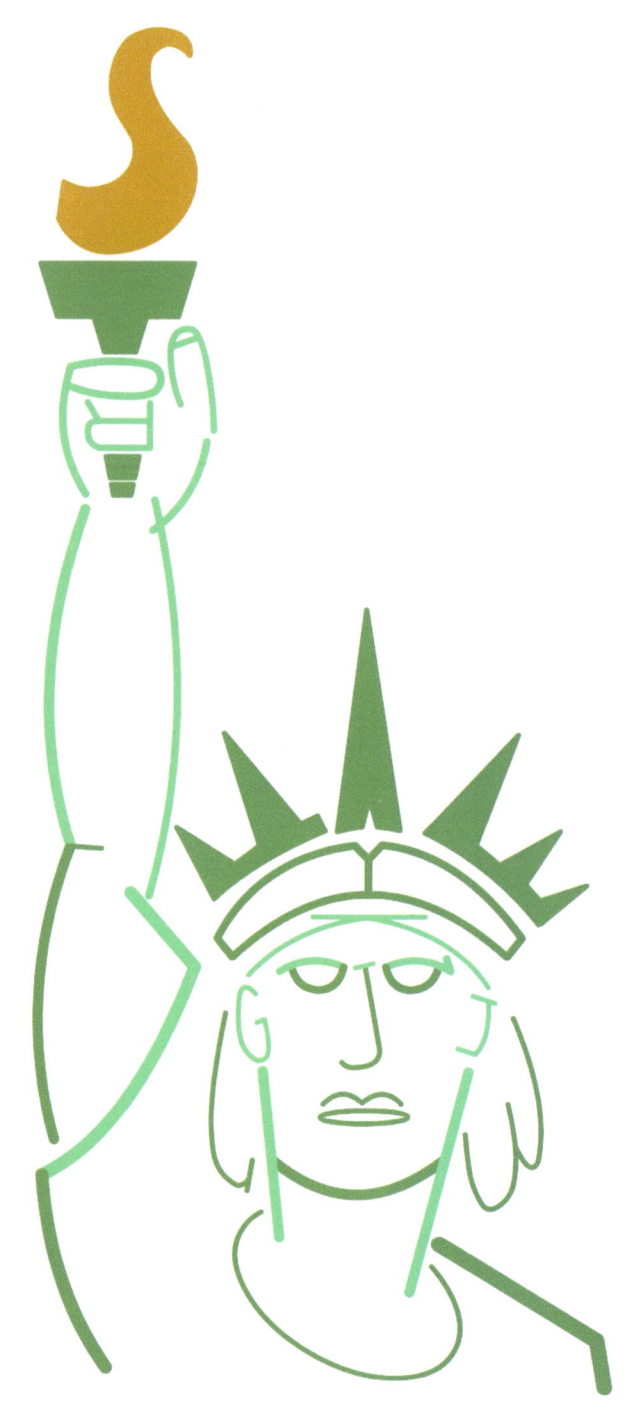

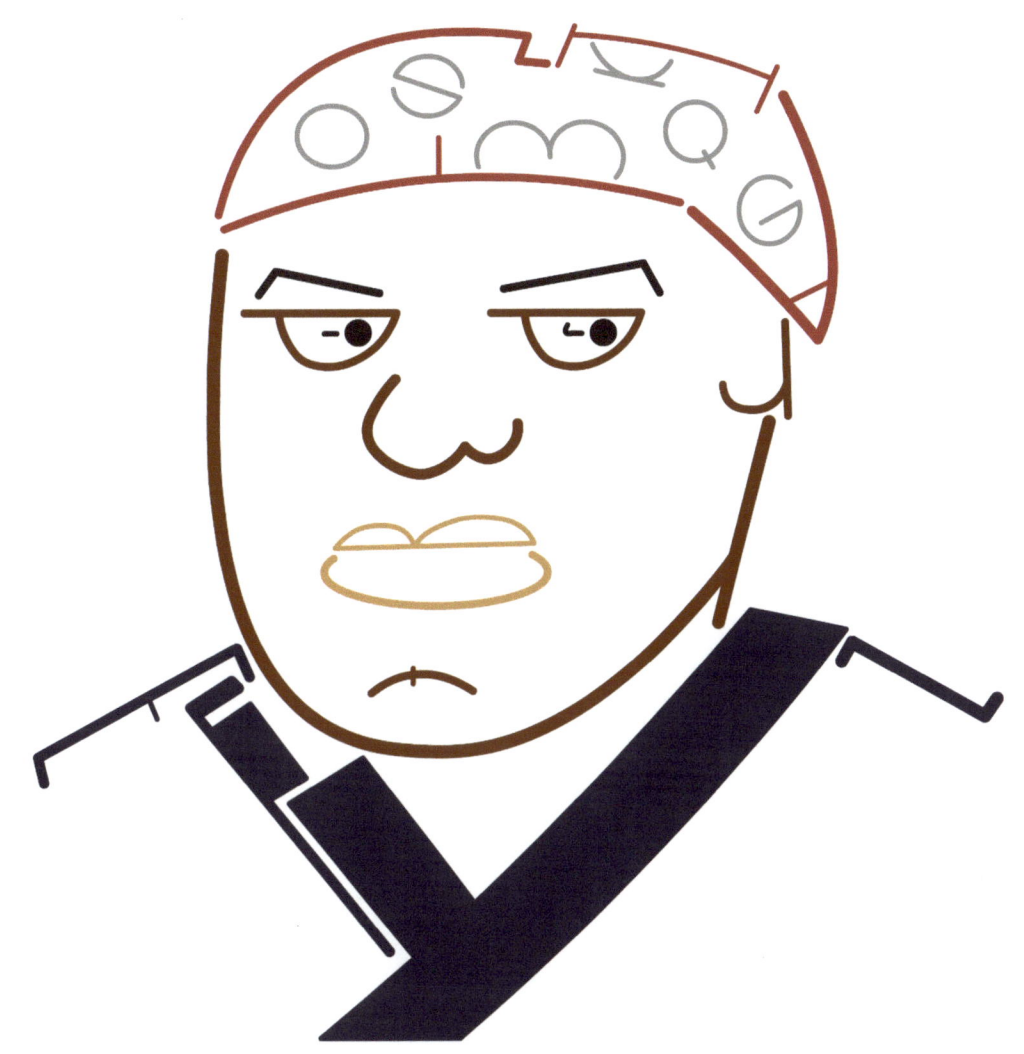

T is for Harriet Tubman,
A woman full of bravery.
She led the Underground Railroad
In the battle against slavery.

U is for
    Uncle
    Sam.

His poster
    says "I
    Want You!"

He reminds
    us to love
    our country

And support
    it through and
    through.

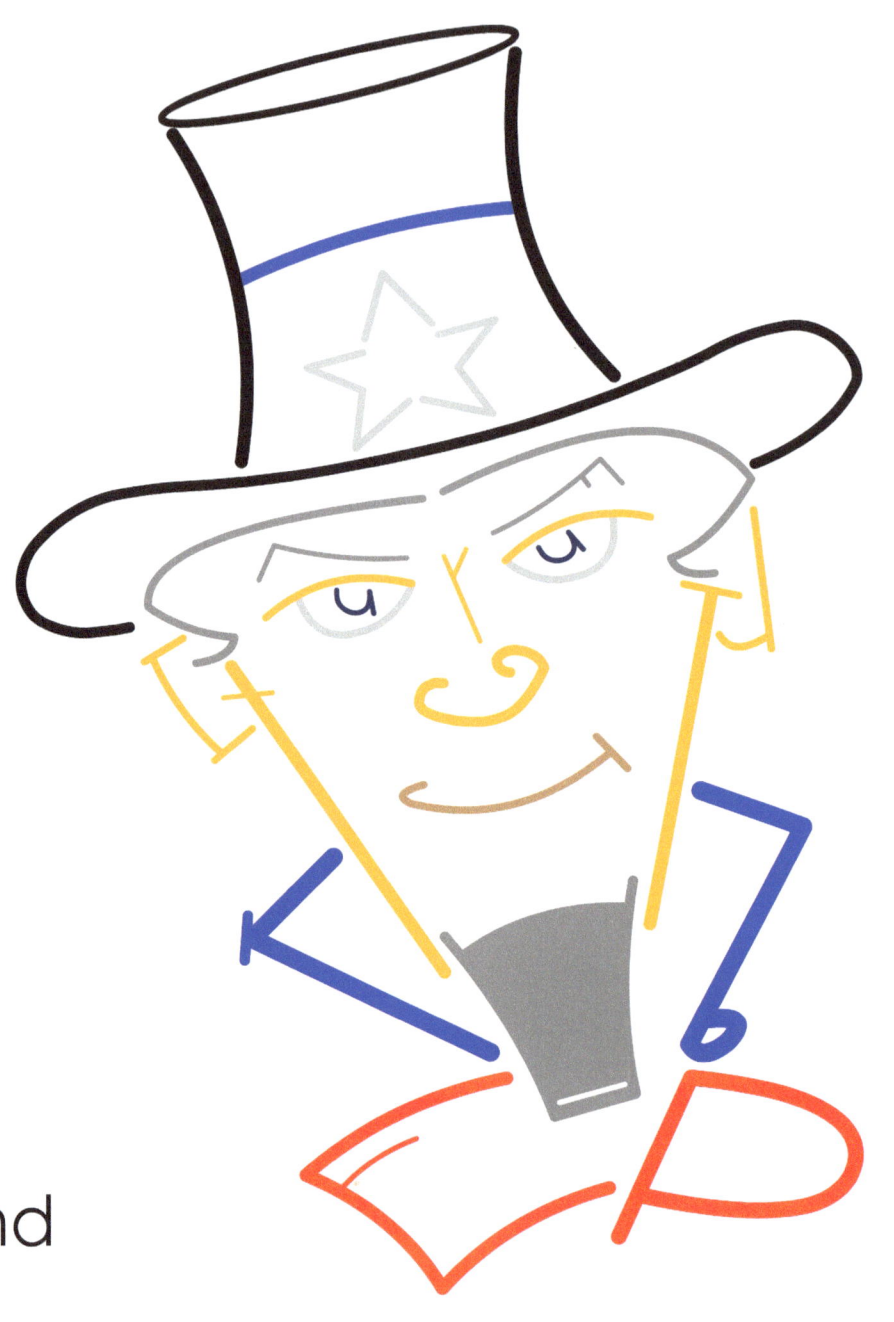

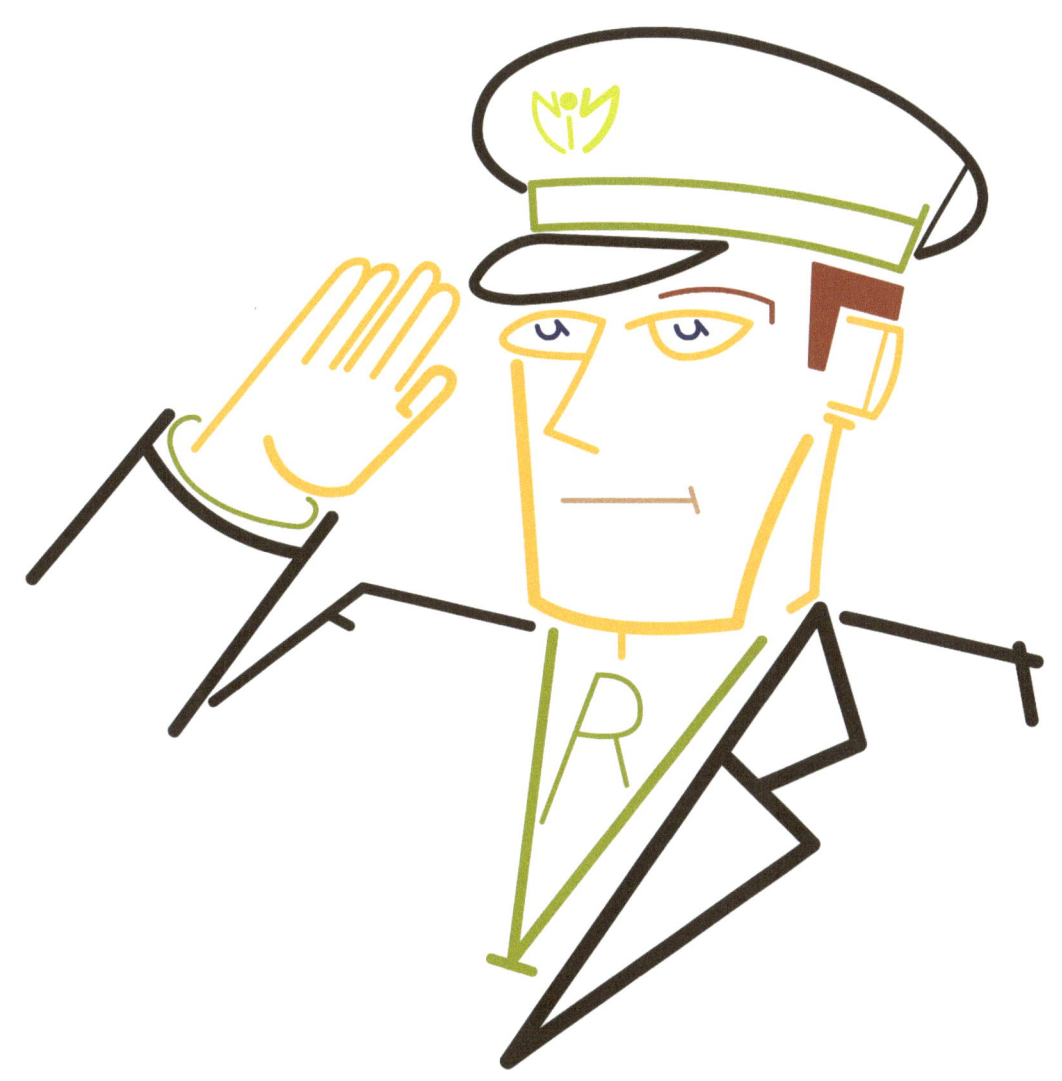

V is for the Veterans
Who served in our military.
Always respect their courage
And the values that they carry.

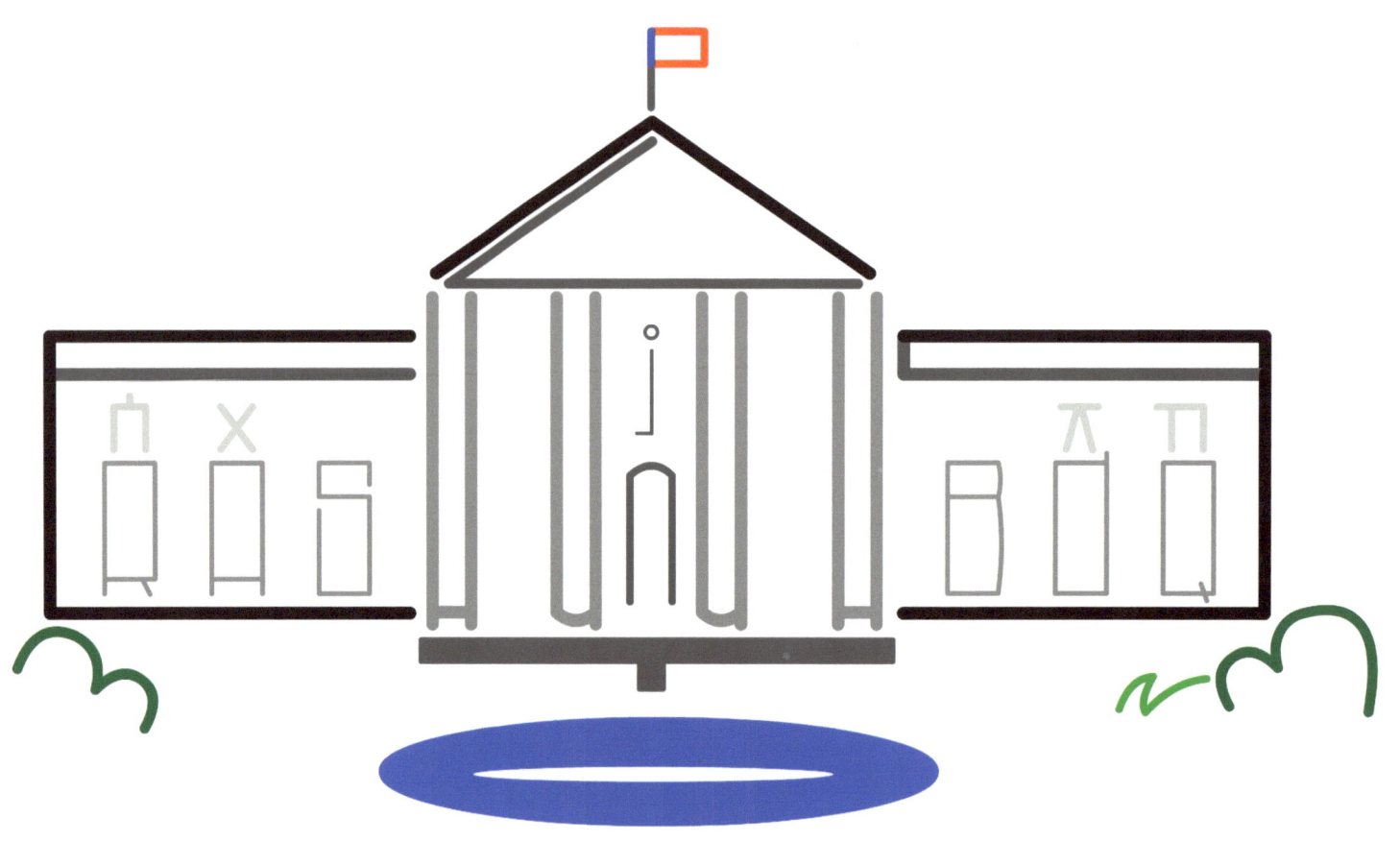

W is for the White House
Where the President resides.
It's on Pennsylvania Avenue,
And the Oval Office is inside.

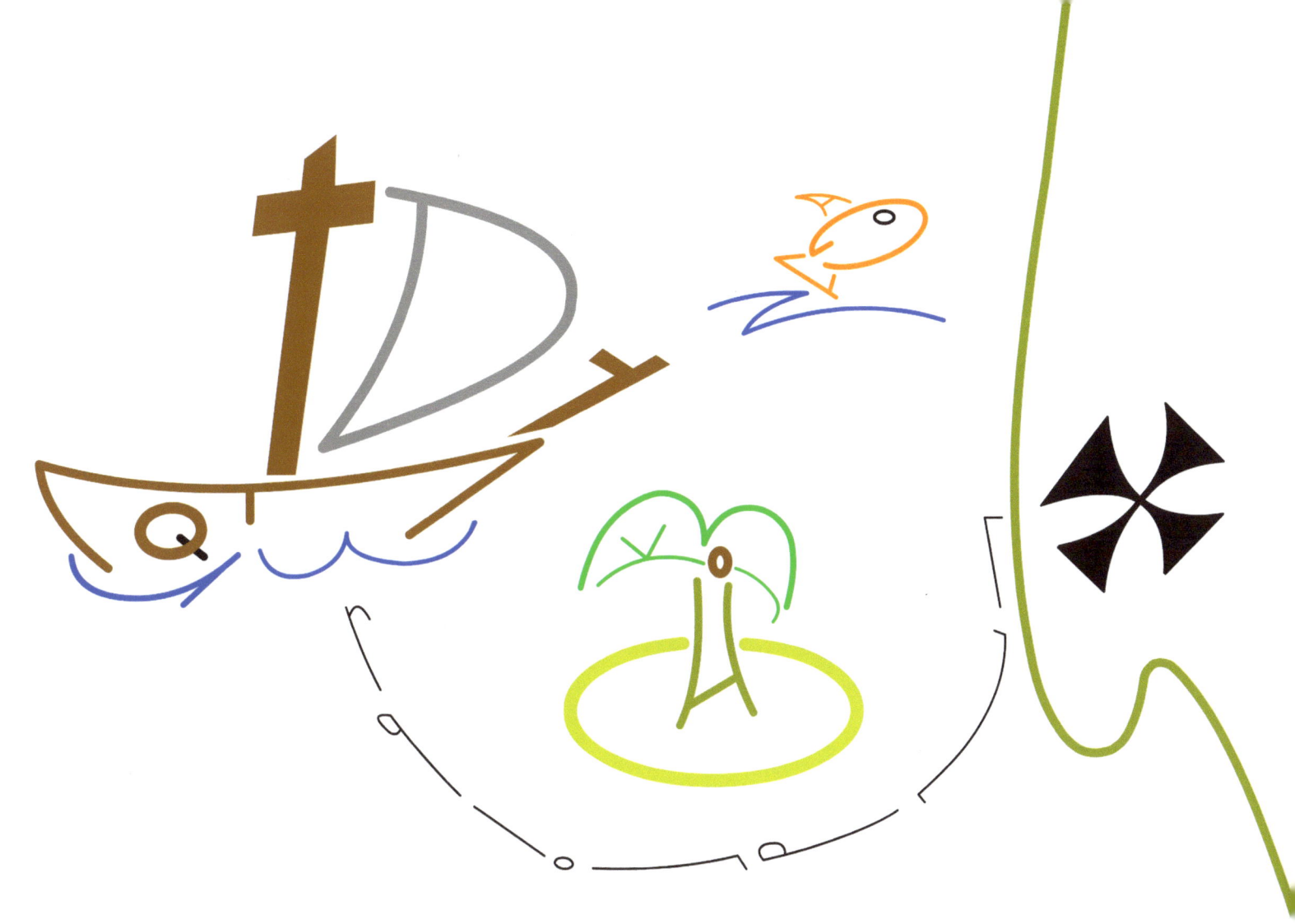

X is for "X Marks the Spot."
On a map, it's the destination.
Travel there and plant your flag
Like the first settlers of our nation.

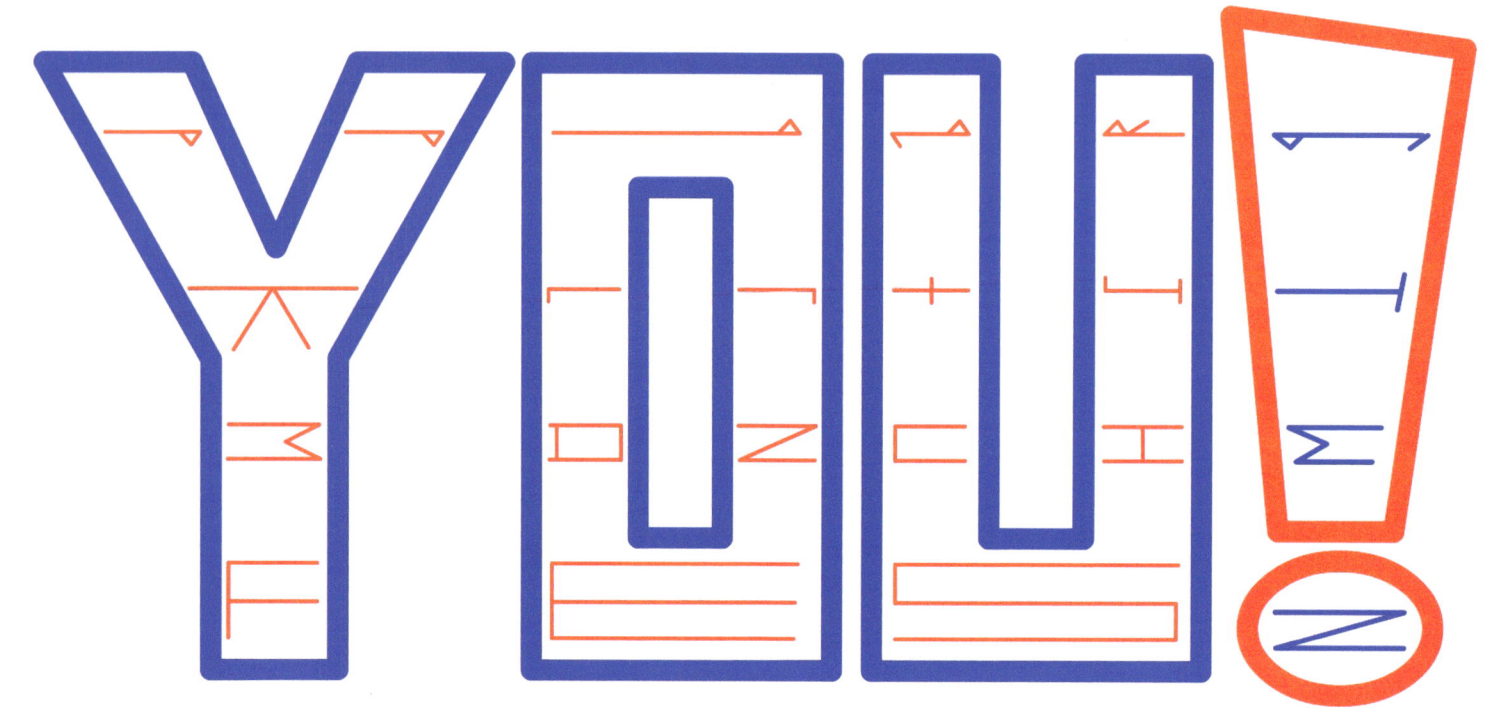

Y is for You
And your place in this story.
Follow your American Dream
To find happiness and glory.

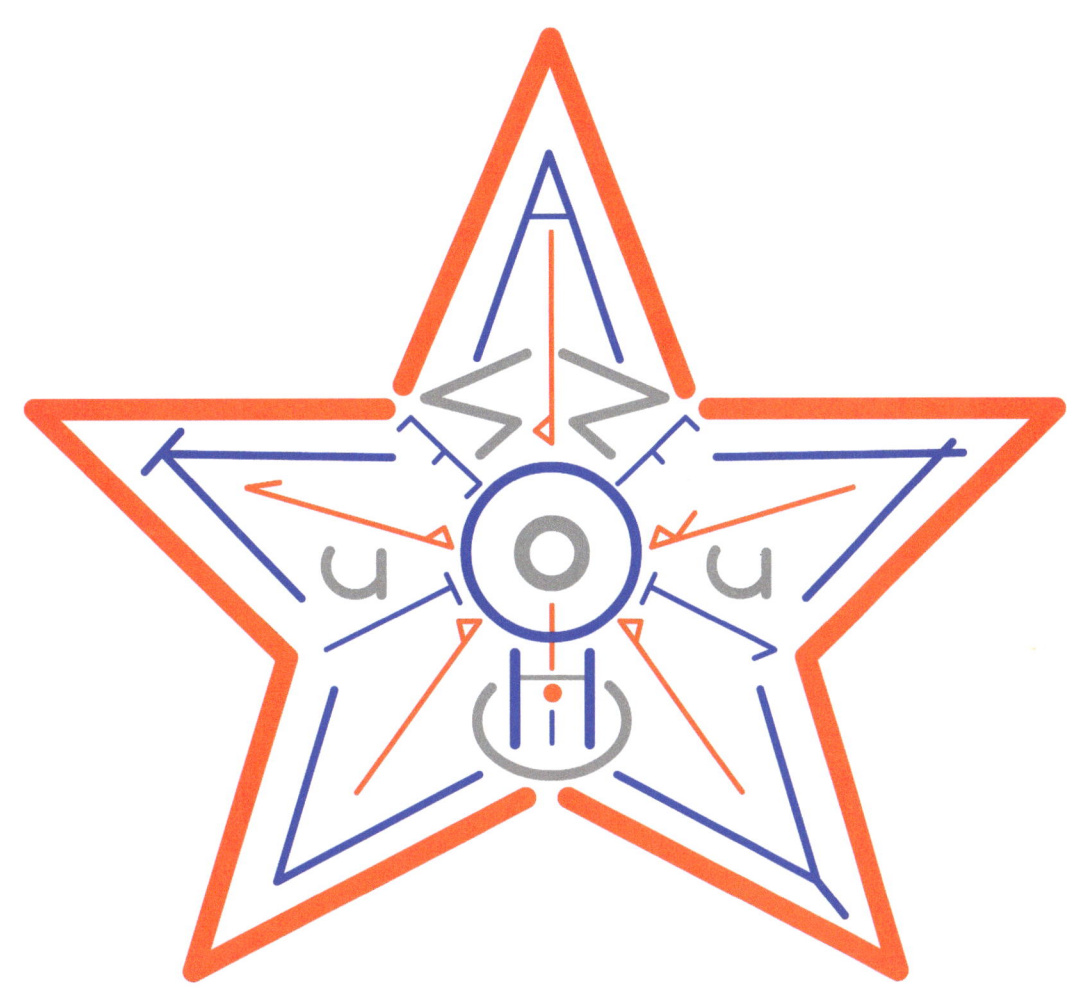

Z is for Zeal,
A special kind of spirit.
It helps make America great!
You'll know it when you're near it.

LETTER LOCATIONS

Alpha-Sketch drawings are made entirely with the alphabet. Each letter appears only once. There are no omissions, repetitions, or extra lines. At times, it may appear as if a letter is used twice. This is due to how similar some letters are. For example, "d" and "p" are the same symbol, only rotated. The following pages reveal the letters' locations.

If you enjoyed this book, I would welcome an online review. Check out braddparton.com for the latest releases, information on school visits, and more. Thanks for reading!

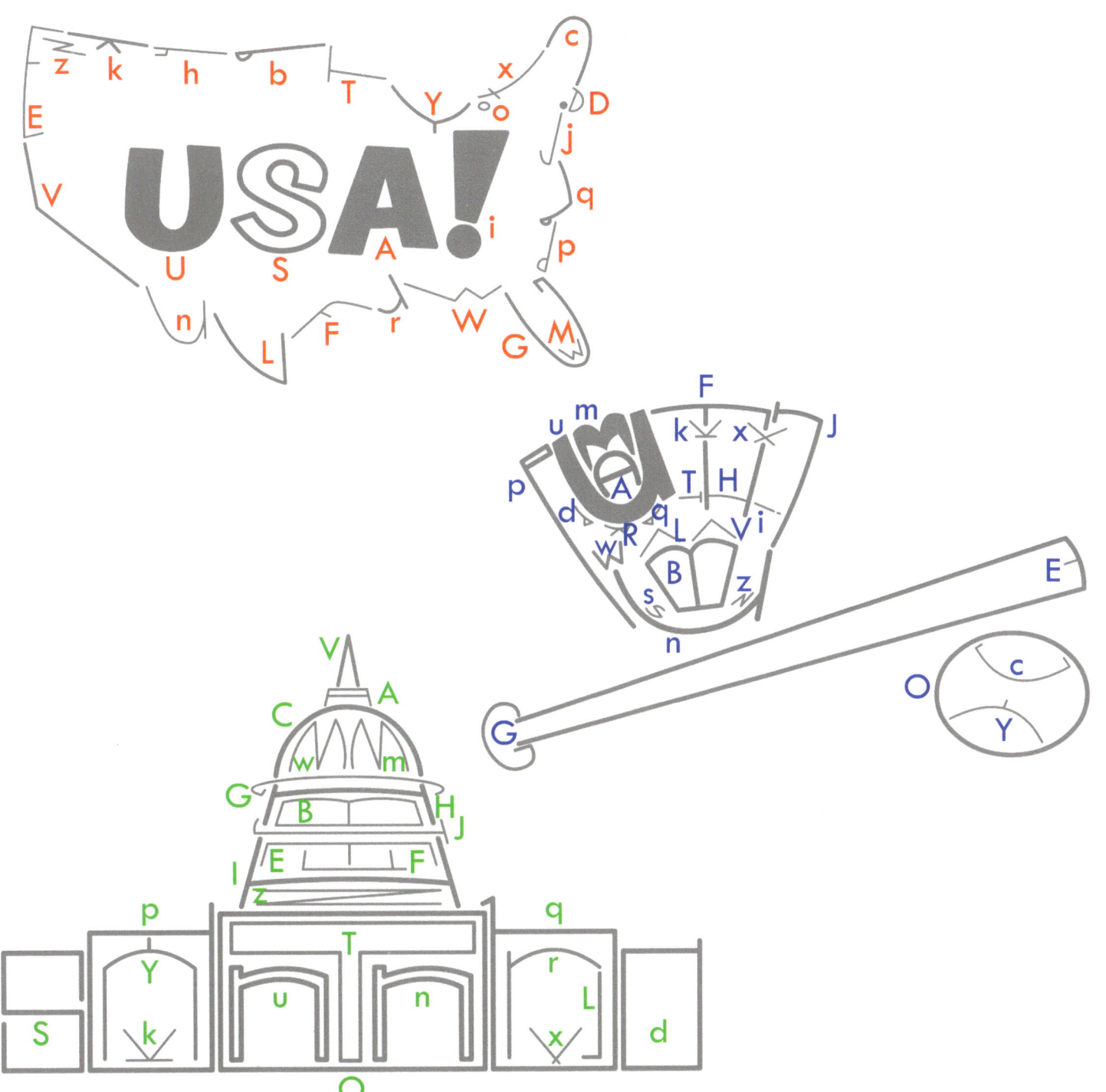

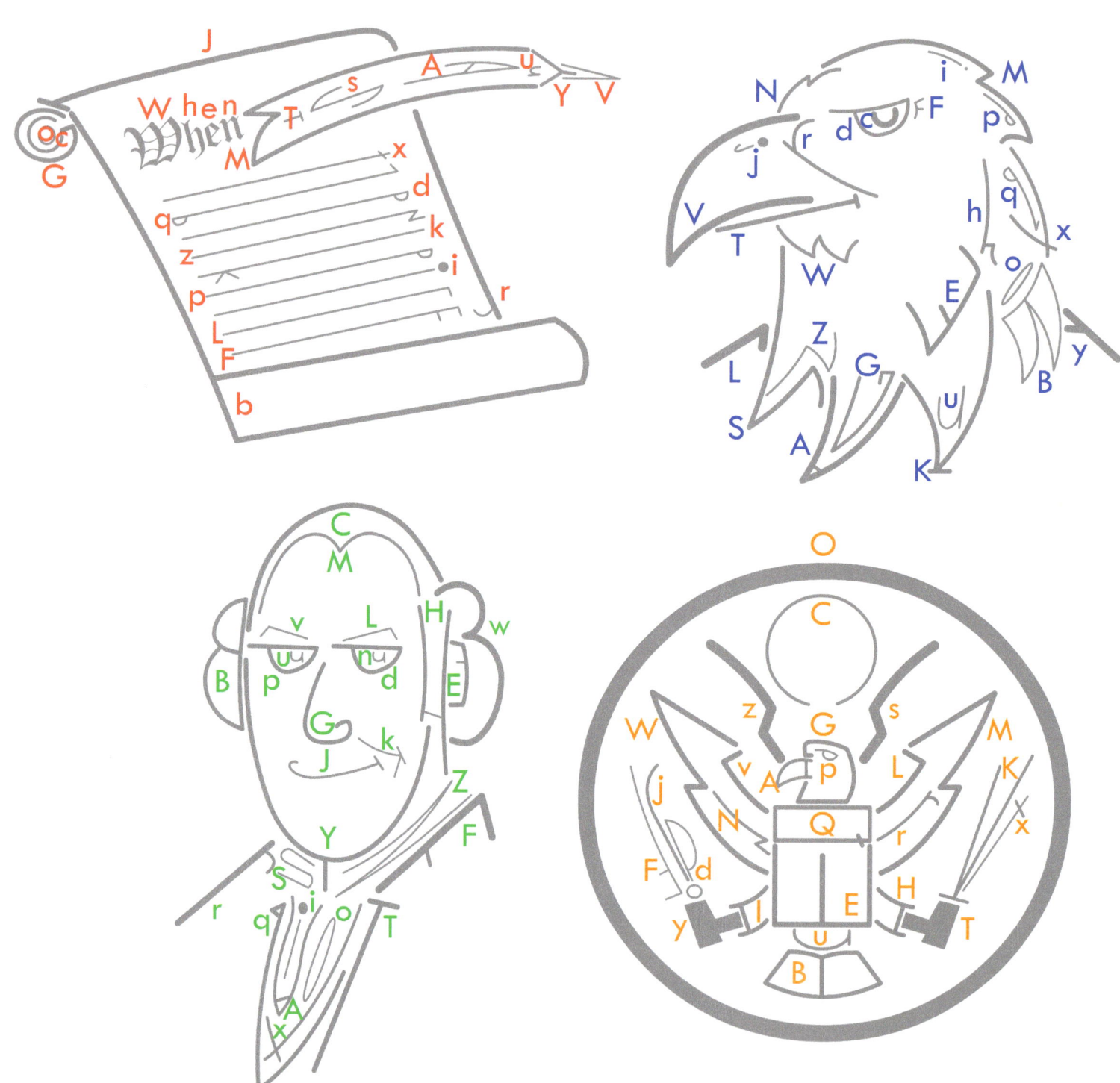

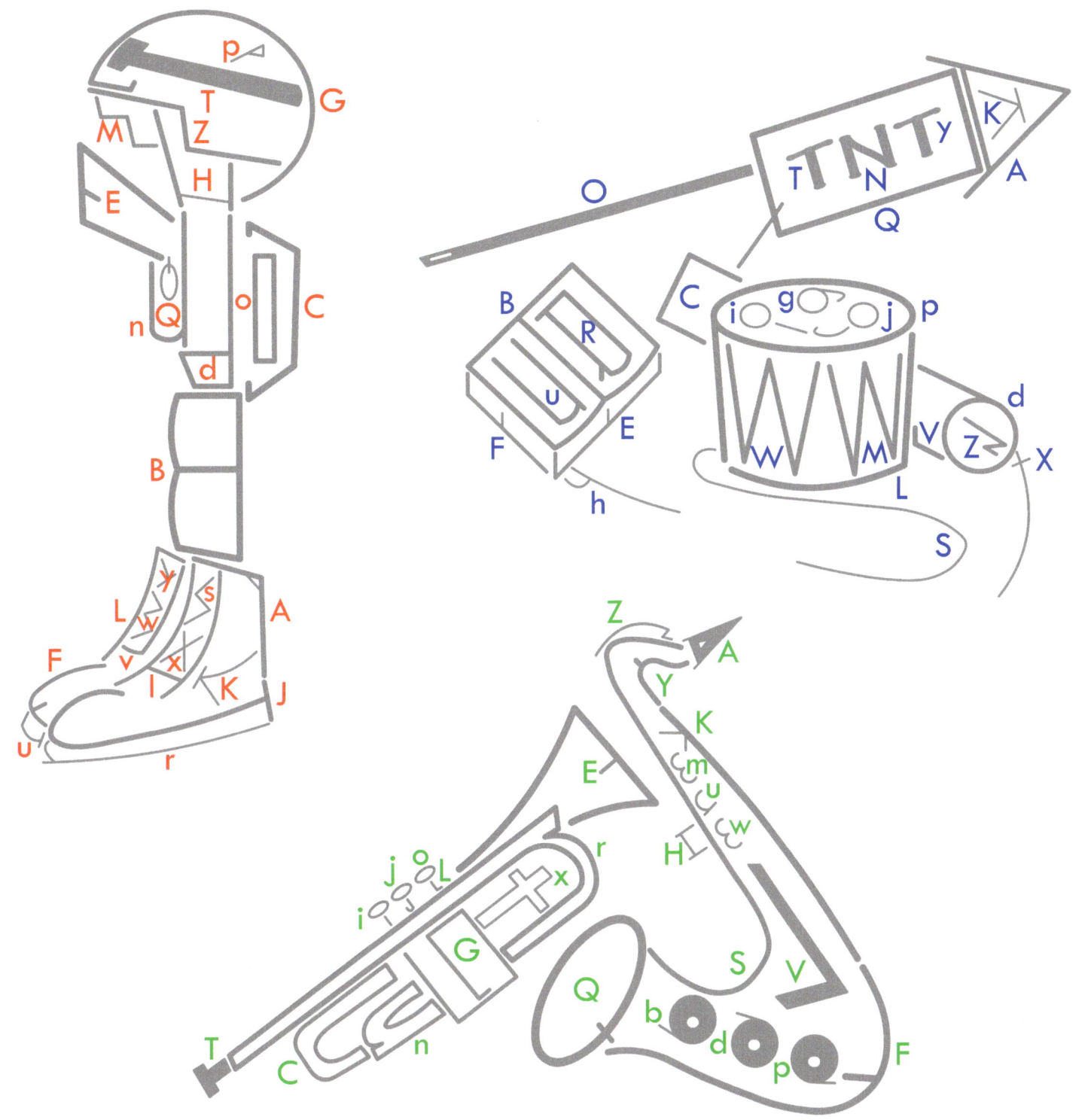

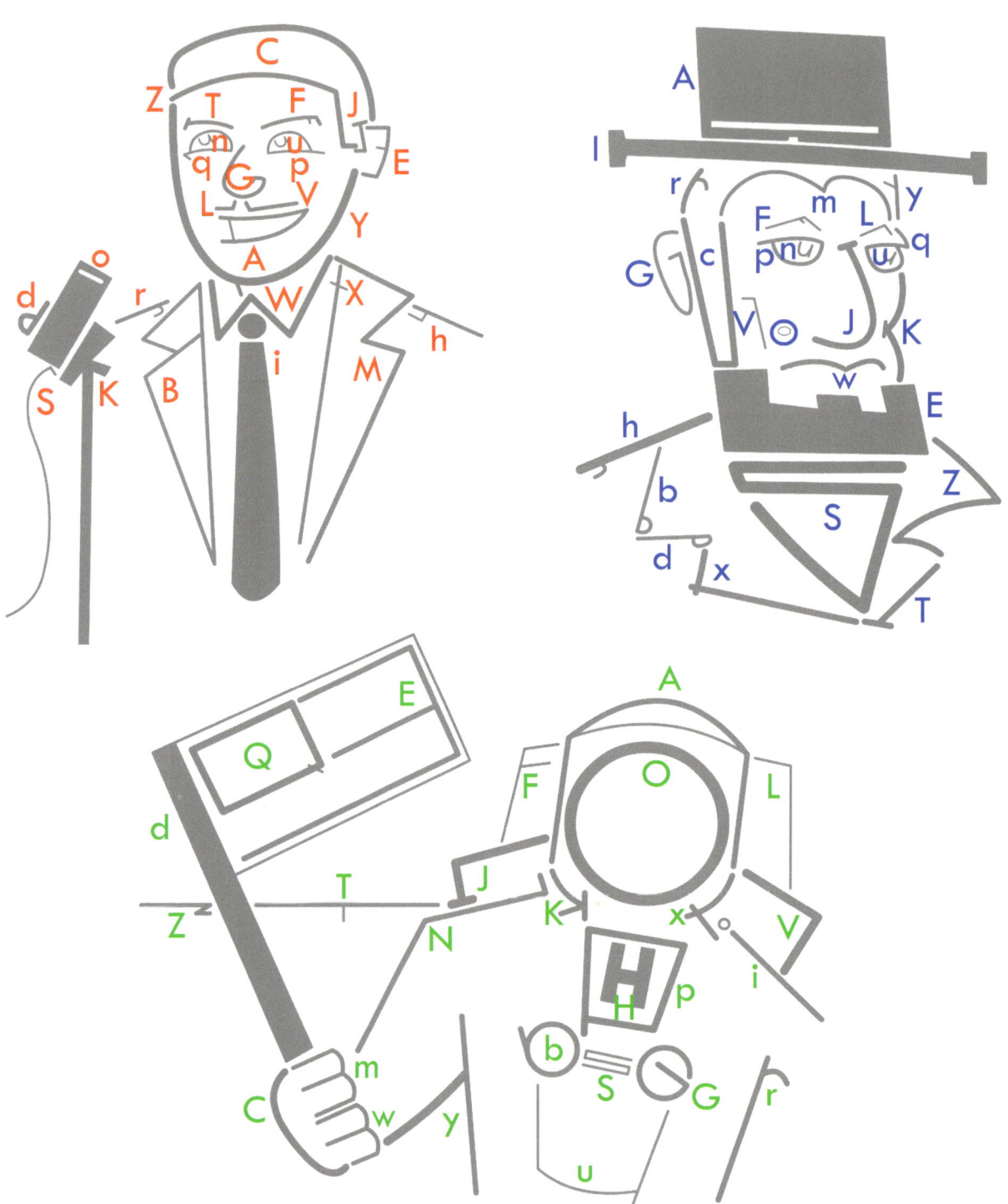

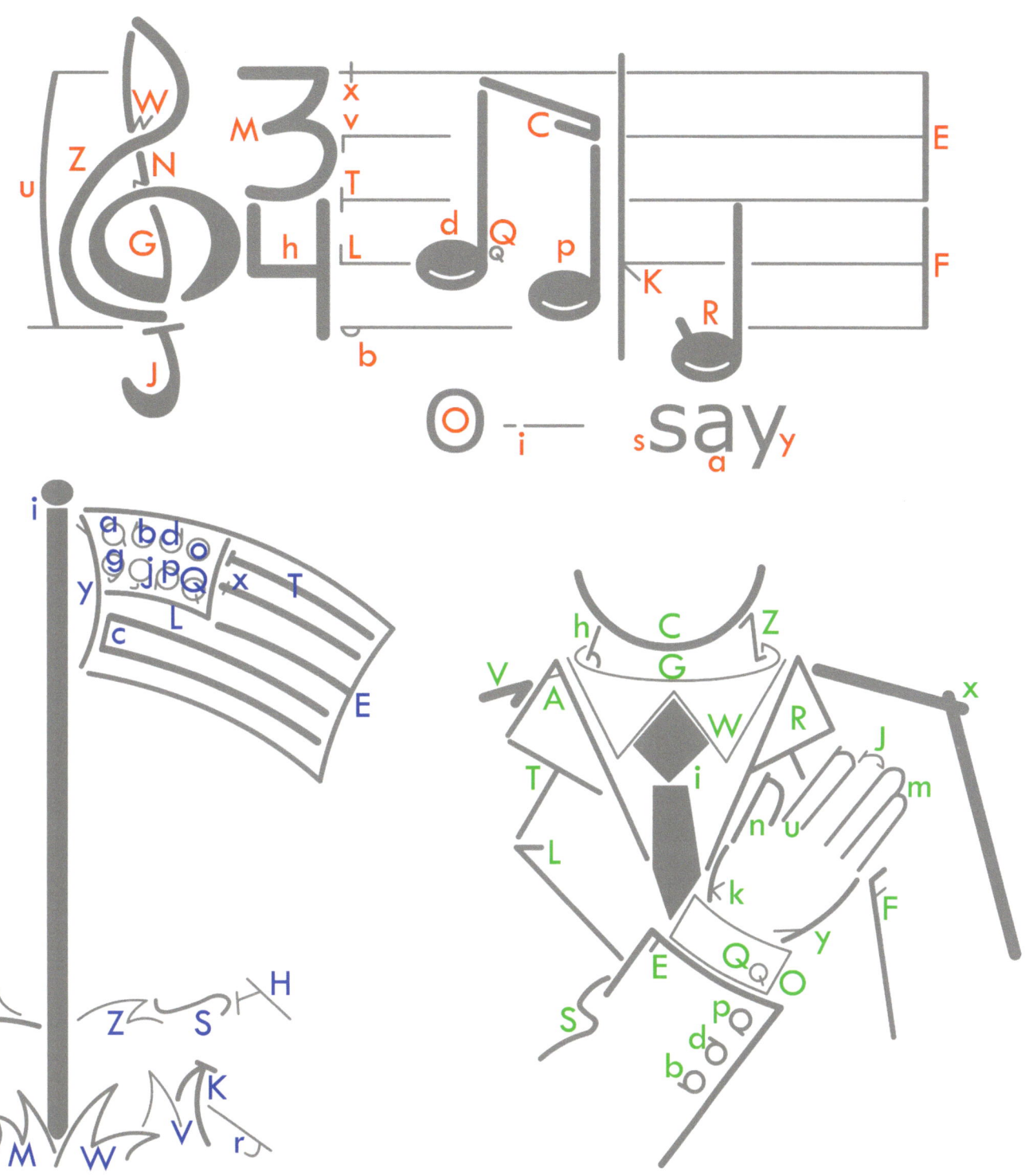

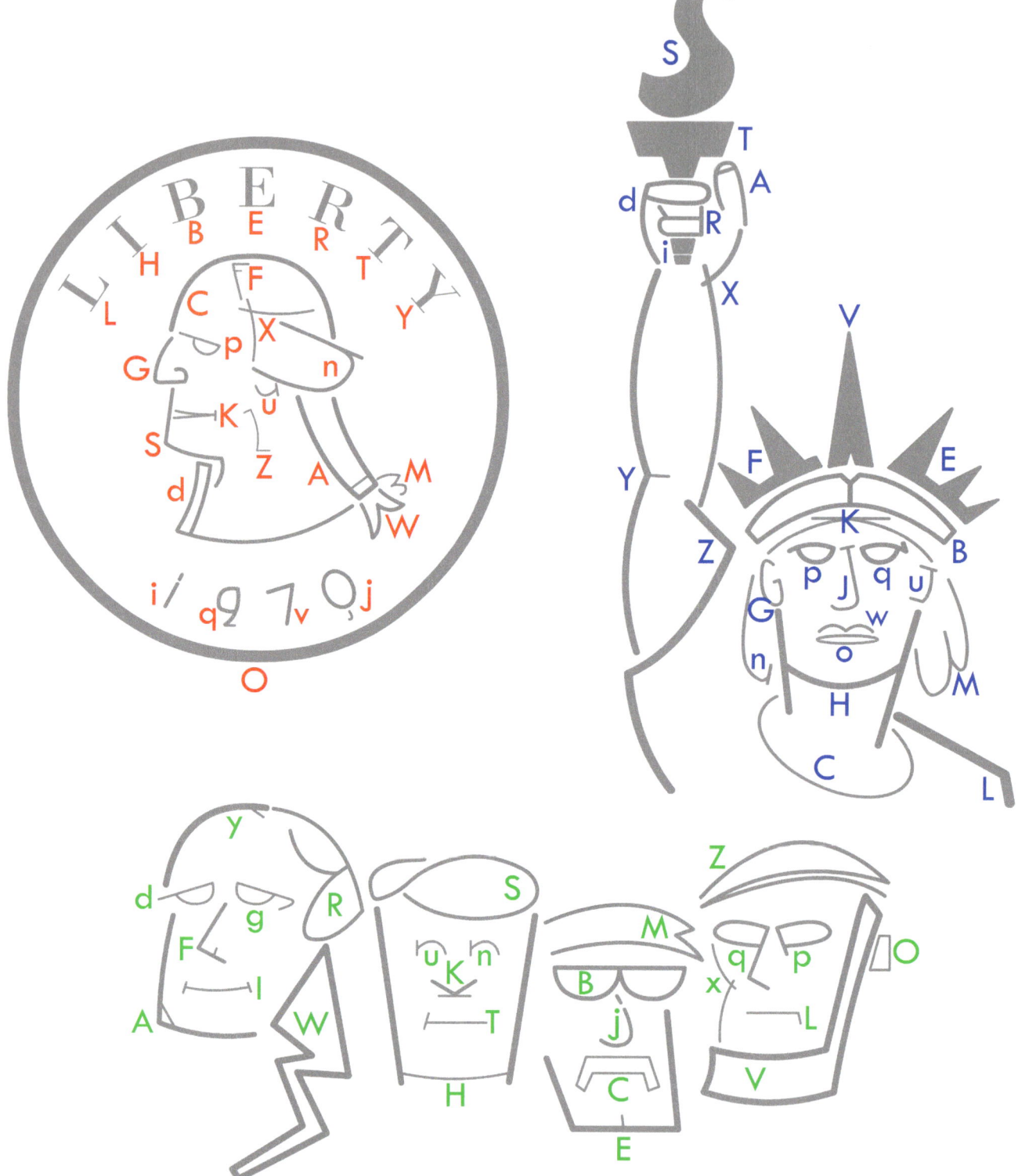

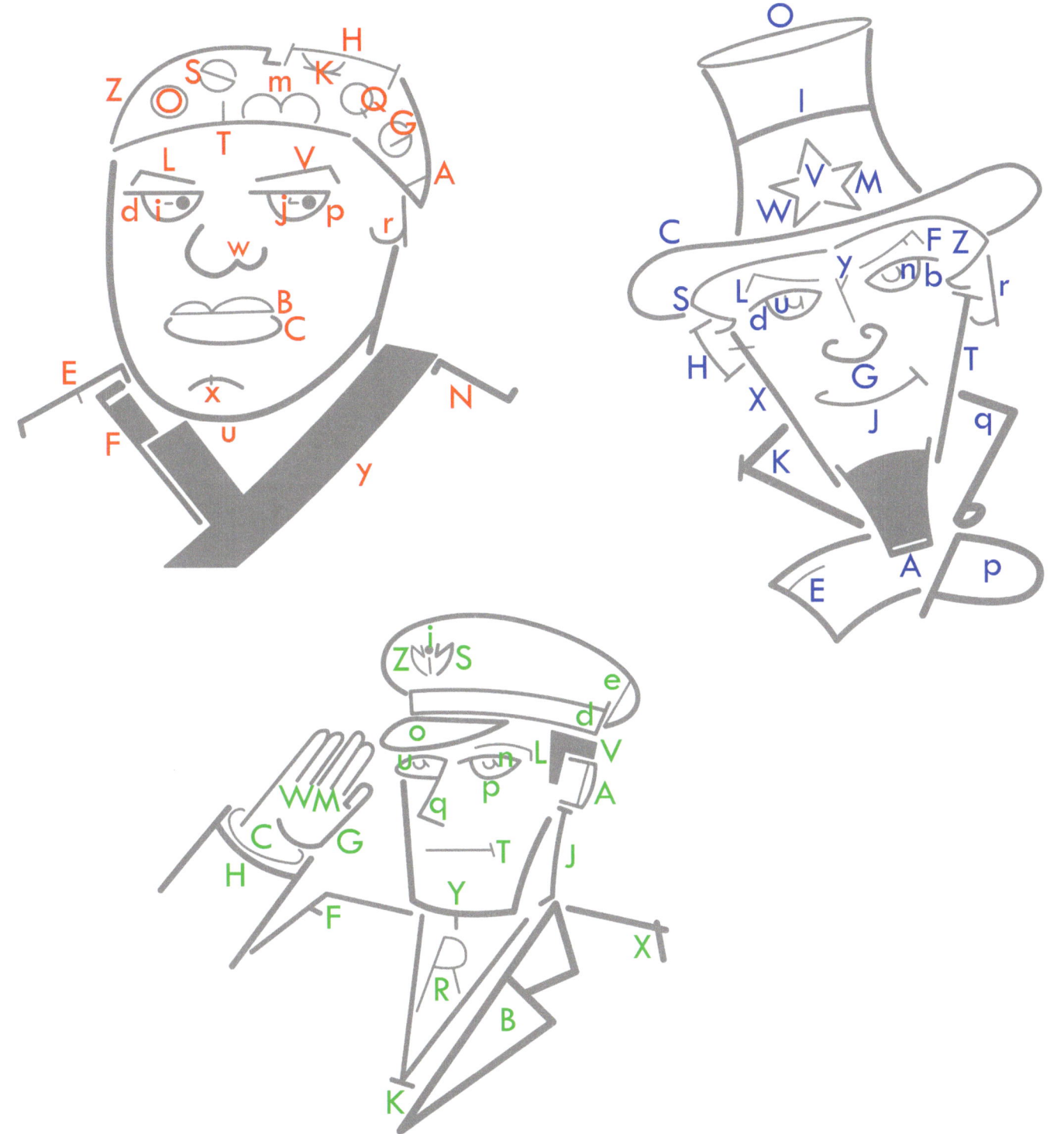

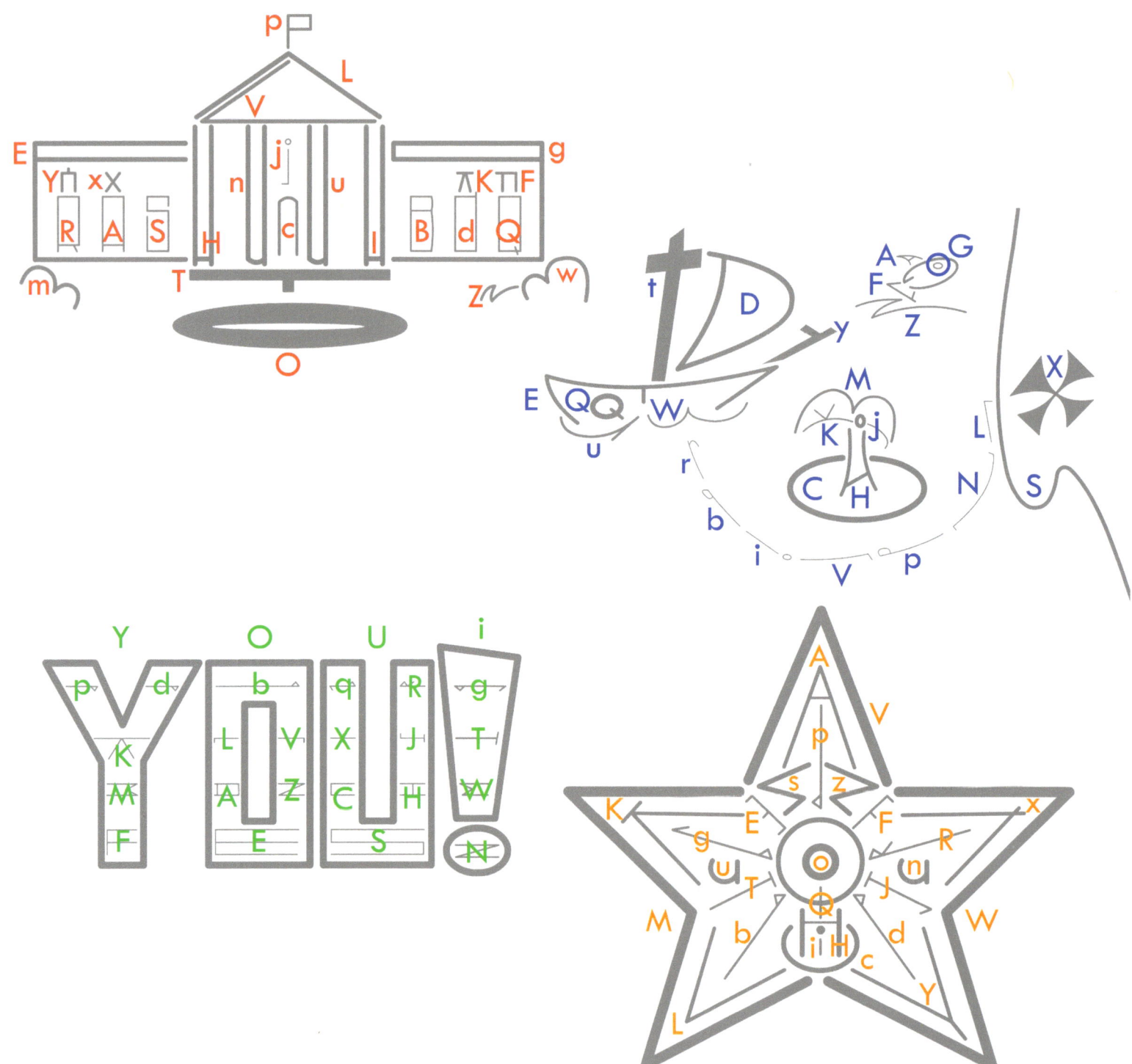

www.ingramcontent.com/pod-product-compliance
Lightning Source LLC
Chambersburg PA
CBHW040453220526
45473CB00004B/1626